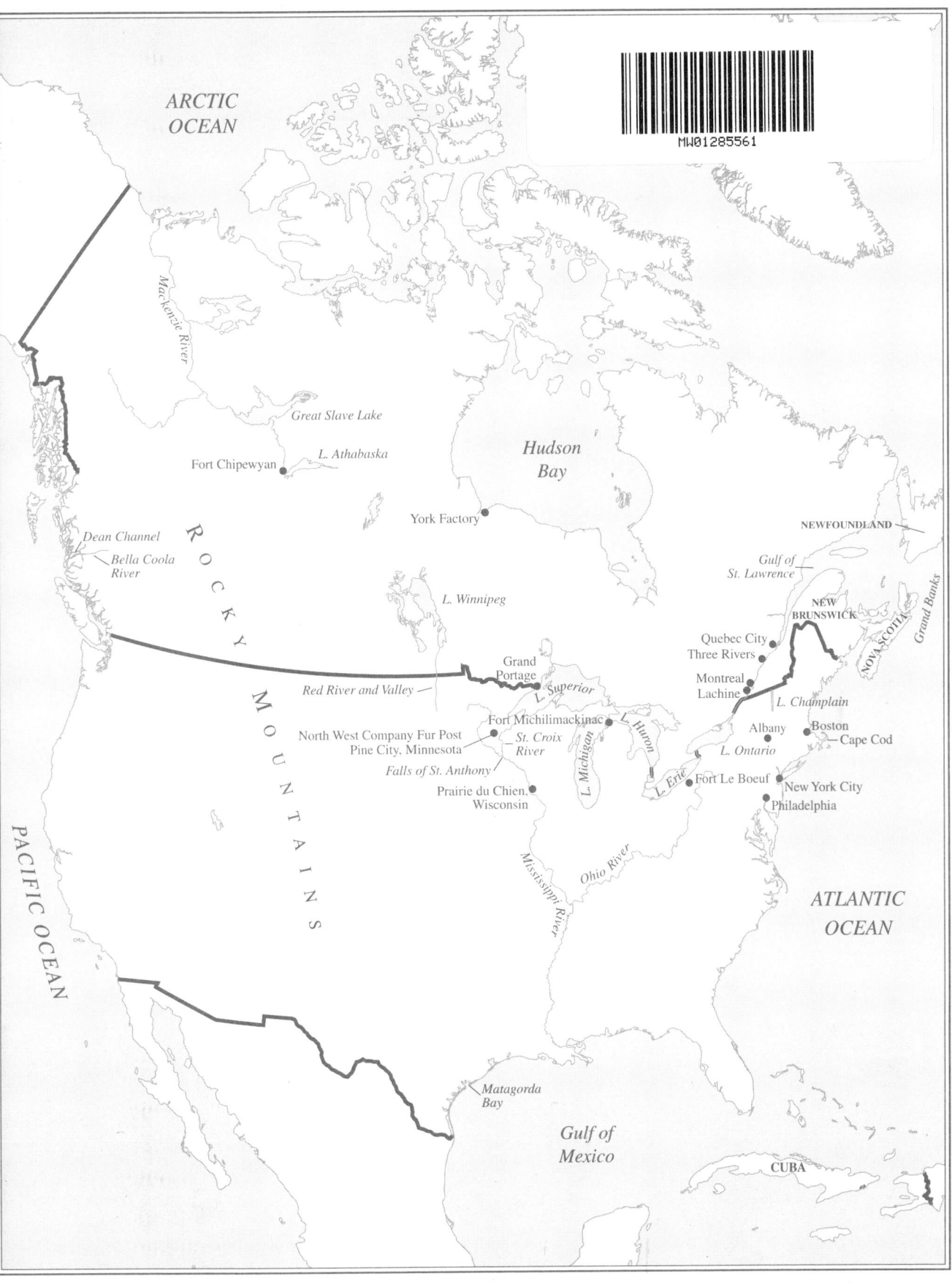

ARCTIC
OCEAN

Mackenzie River

Great Slave Lake

Fort Chipewyan *L. Athabaska*

Hudson
Bay

York Factory

NEWFOUNDLAND

Dean Channel

*Bella Coola
River*

R
O
C
K
Y

*Gulf of
St. Lawrence*

NEW
BRUNSWICK

L. Winnipeg

Quebec City
Three Rivers

NOVA SCOTIA

Grand Banks

Grand
Portage

Montreal
Lachine

Red River and Valley

L. *Superior*

L. Champlain

M
O
U
N
T
A
I
N
S

Fort Michilimackinac

North West Company Fur Post
Pine City, Minnesota

*St. Croix
River*

Albany

Boston

Cape Cod

L. Michigan

L. Huron

L. Ontario

Falls of St. Anthony

Prairie du Chien,
Wisconsin

L. *Erie*

Fort Le Boeuf

New York City
Philadelphia

Mississippi River

Ohio River

ATLANTIC
OCEAN

PACIFIC OCEAN

*Matagorda
Bay*

Gulf of
Mexico

CUBA

BIRCHBARK BRIGADE

BIRCHBARK
A FUR TRADE HISTORY
BRIGADE

Cris Peterson

CALKINS CREEK
Honesdale, Pennsylvania

Library of Congress Cataloging-in-Publication Data
Peterson, Cris.
Birchbark brigade : a fur trade history / Cris Peterson.
p. cm.
Includes bibliographical references and index.
ISBN 978-1-59078-426-6 (hardcover : alk. paper)
1. Frontier and pioneer life—North America—Juvenile literature. 2. Fur trade—
North America—History—Juvenile literature. 3. Fur traders—North America—History—
Juvenile literature. 4. Pioneers—North America—History—Juvenile literature. 5. Explorers—
North America—History—Juvenile literature. 6. Indians of North America—History—
Juvenile literature. 7. North America—Discovery and exploration—Juvenile literature.
8. North America—History—Juvenile literature. I. Title.
E46.P48 2009
970.01—dc22
2008055109

Endsheets: Mapping Specialists, Ltd., Madison, Wisconsin

CALKINS CREEK
An Imprint of Boyds Mills Press, Inc.
815 Church Street
Honesdale, Pennsylvania 18431

10 9 8 7 6 5 4 3 2

CONTENTS

ACKNOWLEDGMENTS

The best part of writing a book is collaborating with dozens of helpful, enthusiastic, and patient people. I'd like to first thank my incredibly patient husband, Gary, for losing most of his farm office over the past four years to books, maps, and dozens of rewrites of this manuscript. Thanks also to Carolyn P. Yoder, my ever-forbearing editor, who took hours of many days to walk me through the process of revising and clarifying my passionate vision of the fur trade that somehow was lost out there in the north woods with the beavers! This book is as much hers as mine. Patrick Schifferdecker, site manager of the North West Company Fur Post in Pine City, Minnesota, read my manuscript twice and offered suggestions and clarifications that only an expert in the subject could. Pam Neil, chief of interpretation at Grand Portage National Monument, graciously provided crucial help sourcing important images for the book. I thank my agent and good friend, Karen Klockner, for encouraging me to pursue my love for history and for being so supportive of my writing over many years. And I can't forget the librarians at Grantsburg Public Library, especially Kim Hinrichs, who acquired ancient, dusty books via intralibrary loan over and over again. There are several tomes I ordered three or four times. I probably should have bought them. Thanks to my brother, Bill Hoeppner, for his beautiful photos of the fur post and expertise on ancient guns. And thanks to Joe Neubauer for taking time to tell me his marvelous story of discovering the North West Company Fur Post in Pine City, Minnesota, as a young boy. I couldn't have dreamed up a more perfect ending to my book.

For my brother, Bill Hoeppner

September 29, 1961

When the author, Cris Peterson, was young, she and her father, Bill Hoeppner, enjoyed fishing on the rivers and lakes of northern Wisconsin. Here, they are sailing on Big Wood Lake when the author was ten years old.

PREFACE

When I was young, my father took my brother and me fishing on the St. Croix River, a meandering wilderness river bordering Minnesota and Wisconsin. We'd motor upstream in our old aluminum boat as far as Nelson's Landing. Then Dad would cut the engine and we'd cast our lines. As we drifted south and fished for smallmouth bass and trout, Dad told us stories of the river before motor boats, before the loggers, even before the United States was a country.

His stories about the fur trade, with its birchbark canoes and daring French voyageurs, made it difficult to concentrate on catching fish. The idea that explorers, traders, and Indians had possibly camped on the same island where I dug my toes into the sand captured my imagination. At every rocky outcrop or bend in the river, I'd wonder who from the past had seen this, where they were from, what they had thought of this wilderness land. For me, history wasn't dusty old dates and boring details. History was alive in the air, the water, and surrounding earth.

Ten years later, when a two-hundred-year-old fur-trading post site was excavated only a few miles from where we used to fish, archaeologists and historians dug up historical evidence of what I had heard about in my dad's stories. As the North West Company Fur Post on the Snake River was carefully rebuilt, musket balls, arrowheads, and axes from two centuries ago were unearthed, and the information they revealed helped bring a long-forgotten story to life. The fort's reconstruction further encouraged my fascination with this obscure part of America's history.

Today, when I cross a bridge over a wilderness stream in northwest Wisconsin, I can almost see the fur traders and Indians in their canoes, paddling around the same bends in the river that stretch before me. When the lakes freeze over and the woods are blanketed with snow, I imagine them in their log-cabin fur posts, waiting for the spring thaw. And when the Canada geese begin their honking migration back to the lakes and ponds near our farm, they remind me that I still live on the edge of a wilderness that was inhabited by the traders long ago.

INTRODUCTION

Today, in the woodlands of Canada and the northern United States, pine boughs whisper to one another, and aspen leaves rattle in the breeze. A maze of shimmering lakes and streams stretches in all directions. And ghostly white birch trees stand like sentinels guarding a really great story from the past.

It doesn't look like much from the road. Thick woods march right up to the asphalt in many places. An occasional bridge over a stream gives you a glimpse beyond the wall of green. Bears, moose, and deer wander just out of sight. Fish swirl in the streams, beavers build dams and munch on the aspen, and loons whistle and dance on the waters of countless sparkling lakes. There are still thousands of square miles of wilderness across North America.

It is the same wilderness the first European explorers encountered when they found their way west from the Atlantic Ocean more than five hundred years ago.

The streams teemed with fish of every sort. Countless beavers—huge flat-tailed rodents that had been hunted to near extinction in Europe by 1500—built mud-and-stick lodges on the edges of ponds and in the backwaters of nearly every river.

The Indians who lived here knew how to survive and even thrive in this land that seemed so untamed and inhospitable to the Europeans. The Indians hunted wild game and built

Weighing in at between thirty and sixty pounds, beavers are the largest rodents in North America. At the height of the fur trade in the 1700s, one estimate put their population at about 150 million.

A few skilled artisans still create birchbark canoes today. Here, park ranger Erik Simula, a master canoe builder, is constructing one at Grand Portage National Monument assisted by summer youth ranger David Riehm.

shelters of bark, moss, and branches. They trapped the plentiful beavers and used their skins for clothing. Many tribes moved about with the seasons, gathering what they needed to survive. Others farmed, while still others fished or traded. They spoke dozens of different languages.

Without metal tools or weapons, they lived in what would be considered the Stone Age. Before the Europeans arrived, Indian tools for chopping, pounding, drilling, fishing, sewing, and hunting were made of stone, wood, or bone. But after contact with the first explorers who carried metal knives and had iron and brass pots and tools, the Indians recognized the utility of the new items. Stone axes, bone needles or awls, and wooden bowls couldn't compare with the durability of the new iron tools. The Indians traded the furs they wore for "hatchets, knives, scissors, needles, and a steel to strike fire with," wrote one trader. "They all take these instruments from the *Europeans* and reckon the hatchets and knives much better than those which they formerly made of stones and bones."

The fur trade, where the Indians traded furs to the Europeans for tools, kettles, and cloth, lasted for more than three hundred years. That trading, which took place on the rocky banks of the rivers, lakes, and tiny streams just inland from the Atlantic, began a business that unrolled the map of America. It took place in Canada, along the Atlantic seaboard, down the Mississippi River, across the Great Plains of the American West, in the Rocky Mountains, and along the Pacific coast. It involved Europeans from half a dozen countries and dozens of Indian tribes. They used ships, dugout canoes, flat-bottomed boats, mules or oxen hitched to carts, dogs hitched to sleds, men on foot, and men on horseback to transport trade goods inland and furs from the wilderness.

But the most remarkable transportation device used by the Indians and the fur traders was the birchbark canoe, a lightweight watercraft created by the tribes in the Great Lakes region. The wilderness area of rocks, trees, and rivers was nearly impossible to travel except along its many waterways. Fortunately, it was the prime habitat for giant white birch, white cedar, and spruce trees—the building materials for the birchbark canoe.

Made from the tough, leathery outer layer of bark from a large birch tree stretched over a framework of white cedar branches, or ribs, the canoe was sewn and

The birchbark canoe is an engineering marvel built entirely of materials available in the woodlands surrounding the Great Lakes region. Ranger Simula uses freshly peeled slabs of birchbark, cedar staves, and spruce roots to construct his canoe. Here he is lacing the gunwales with spruce roots.

lashed together with spruce roots. The seams between the pieces of birchbark were slathered with a black, gooey pine-pitch concoction to keep the water out.

An empty canoe was lightweight and tippy. It appeared as fragile as an eggshell and floated high in the water like a freshly fallen oak leaf. But loaded up with kegs, crates, bales, and bundles, it carried from three thousand to five thousand pounds of trade goods, not counting people and their supplies, and it floated a mere six inches out of the water.

Adopted by the fur trade as a sort of semitrailer of the wilderness, birchbark canoes were paddled along every lake, river, and stream from eastern Canada to the very heart of what is now the United States. Several of these canoes traveling together were called a brigade.

Birchbark brigades of fur traders bent on making a profit in the wilderness of North America recognized that their business depended on a cooperative relationship with the Indians. The Indians were the ones who trapped the beavers and prepared their skins for shipment to Europe, where the fur was made into hats. The Indians provided fresh meat, wild rice, and other food to the traders, along with a deep knowledge of the wilderness essential to the traders' survival.

By the time the United States won the Revolutionary War and then made George Washington its first president in 1789, the fur trade was at its peak. Brigades of birchbark canoes filled with traders, merchandise, and bales of beaver pelts extended across most of North America. The wilderness west of the British colonies wasn't an empty, unexplored land. It was the home of the biggest business on the continent—the fur trade and its birchbark brigades.

But it all started three hundred years earlier—just as Europe was emerging from the Middle Ages.

CHAPTER 1

"Brandishing Peltry on Sticks"

It all began by accident. Five hundred years ago, maps of the world were missing a whole hemisphere. When explorers first sailed west from Europe, North America was supposed to be China, the mysterious far-off land rich with spices, silks, and gold.

Most Europeans had no idea what lay beyond their own small farms and villages much less beyond the salty ocean waters to the west. They focused on scraping together a living on their hardscrabble farms, where a smoky, one-room hut with walls of clay and a thatched roof served as home. Or they lived in noisy, stench-filled cities, where church bells clanged, vendors hawked their wares on the streets, and horse carts constantly clattered on the cobblestones. People back then weren't thinking about new worlds or new anything. And they certainly weren't thinking about furs from a new world.

But Europe was on the edge of a whole new era. A few decades earlier, a goldsmith by the name of Johannes Gutenberg had invented the printing press. By 1490, printing presses were in operation all over Europe, and with so many different kinds of books suddenly available, change slowly tiptoed into every aspect of European life. People seemed to wake up, look around, and decide that life had many more possibilities. Some started painting pictures or climbing mountains just for the fun of it. Others looked to science and exploration to satisfy this sudden urge

Before Johannes Gutenberg invented the printing press in 1440, books were painstakingly copied by hand. The new movable-type press made books far less expensive to reproduce.

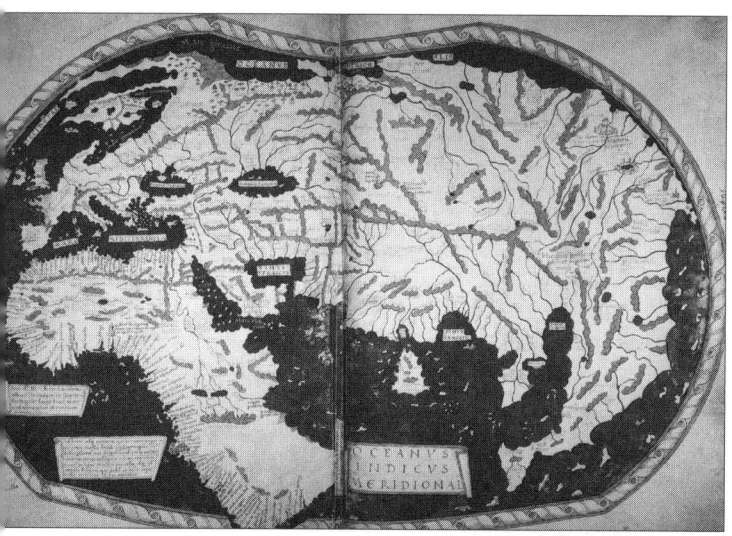

ABOVE Henricus Martellus created his World Map three years before Christopher Columbus discovered the New World. Although Europe is somewhat recognizable, Africa is misshapen and the Western Hemisphere is totally missing.

RIGHT Although no portraits of Christopher Columbus are known to exist, this painting from the 1520s is often identified as a likeness of the famous explorer.

for change. They wondered about the world—its shape and size. This reawakening, or rebirth, would later be called the Renaissance.

Five hundred years ago, maps of the world showed Europe's borders fairly accurately, but only the top one-third of Africa appeared. The outline of Asia was vague, and sometimes its southern tip was drawn connected to an imaginary extension of Africa. That was the whole world back then, surrounded by the vast Ocean Sea.

During this time of new thinking and new exploration, Christopher Columbus set out on a shortcut to China. In 1492, crossing the sea to nowhere was still generally considered an outrageous idea. Most of the royalty of Europe who had enough money to fund such a trip didn't believe the journey was possible. Columbus worked six years to persuade Queen Isabella and King Ferdinand of Spain to fund his voyage west and was successful only because he convinced them he'd find piles of gold at his destination. That prospect greatly appealed to the king and queen because their treasury had been severely depleted by carrying on wars in Europe.

Columbus's goal was to find a route to China that would be simpler and less costly than the treacherous caravan routes from the Far East to Europe. At that time, spices, silks, gold, gems, and tea were hauled seven thousand miles from China to the edge of Europe on a winding, dangerous trade network that came to be called the Silk Road.

China's luxurious silk fabric was highly prized throughout the world, and the country's abundant and precious spices were particularly important to European people in Columbus's day. Ginger, pepper, and cloves were used not only to preserve meat but to disguise the smell of it when it began to spoil—which it often did. When the eastern trade routes occasionally became blocked by regional wars or bad weather, the shortage of spices meant a lot of stinky meat in Europe.

The Silk Road wound through impossible mountain passes and across windy, desolate steppes. Camels and stocky, sure-footed horses loaded with trade goods and accompanied by Chinese government officials and private merchants traveled together from oasis to oasis like the wagon trains of the old American West. They avoided areas known for harboring marauding bandits and skirted the northern edge of the Taklamakan, one of the world's largest sand deserts. Known as the "desert of death," its name meant "go in and never come out."

It was an incredibly difficult and costly journey. Some Portuguese mariners had begun sailing south along Africa's coastline to reach China by water, but that added thousands of miles, even more danger, and many more months to a troublesome trip. So avoiding the seven-thousand-mile trek east and risking a trip west across the Atlantic Ocean seemed like a pretty good bet to Columbus. He was certain he'd find what he was looking for, and he did.

Columbus landed on an island off the coast of Cuba on Friday, October 12, 1492. Referring to himself as "the Admiral," he wrote this passage in his journal: "The Admiral bore the royal standard, and the two captains each a banner of the Green Cross, which all the ships had carried; this contained the initials of the names of the King and Queen each side of the cross, and a crown over each letter. Arrived on shore, they saw trees very green many streams of water, and diverse sorts of fruits."

With Columbus's success, the new route to riches pointed west, and within a few years after that first voyage when he claimed everything he had discovered for Spain, more adventurers and explorers convinced other rulers in Europe to underwrite costly voyages in the same direction. Most still thought the spices and silks of the newly discovered "China" were just around the next bend of the coastline.

This wood engraving, created by A. S. Warren for Ballou's Pictorial Drawing-Room Companion, published in 1855, re-creates the discovery of North America by John Cabot.

John Cabot believed, like Columbus, that China could be reached by sailing west. In 1493, when word of Columbus's successful journey arrived in England, Cabot convinced King Henry VII that England did not have to sit by while the Spaniards helped themselves to Asian riches. Even though Spain supposedly had control of all the newly discovered lands, the king liked Cabot's idea and decided to fund the voyage.

Cabot was certain that it was possible to reach Asia on a more northerly route than Columbus had taken, and in a shorter time. He knew that a degree of longitude was shorter the farther one was from the equator, so the voyage from Europe to China would be shorter at higher latitudes.

On May 2, 1497, Cabot set out with a crew of eighteen men and sailed west from Bristol, England. He had no idea he was beginning what would become a three-hundred-year-long quest to find a western route to China. This illusive route would come to be called the Northwest Passage.

When Cabot finally landed on the rocky coastline of North America a month later, he desperately hoped that the thick woods that hugged the shoreline as far up and down the coast as he could see only extended a short distance inland. Surely one of the many rivers flowing from the interior would lead to his ultimate destination. Maybe there was only a small neck or isthmus of land separating his ship, the *Matthew*, and its tiny crew from the Asian sea and China's riches.

Historians don't agree on the exact location of Cabot's landing. Chances are it was in Nova Scotia or Newfoundland. He and his men "found tall trees of the kind masts are made." And although he wasn't able to report back to the English king the wonders of the Far East, his accounts of codfish in schools so thick they could be scooped up in baskets lowered from the side of his ship soon had fishermen from all over Europe sailing to the fog-shrouded waters called the Grand Banks that lay just off the coast of North America. Cabot could never have imagined the immensity of the land he had discovered.

King Henry VII was impressed enough with Cabot's descriptions of the new land that he awarded "to hym that founde the new Isle" ten pounds, made him an admiral, and agreed to finance a second voyage. Five ships and a collection of would-be settlers led by Cabot left Bristol in May 1498. According to a historian of the time, "John [Cabot] set out in this same year and sailed first to Ireland. Then he set sail towards the west. In the event he is believed to have found the new lands nowhere but on the very bottom of the ocean, to which he is thought to have descended

together with his boat, … since after that voyage he was never seen again anywhere." Apparently after only a few days at sea, four of the five ships sank in a storm and the fifth barely limped back to Ireland.

The loss of Cabot and his ships temporarily dampened English enthusiasm for exploring the New World—the name people had begun to use to describe the lands that lay west across the Atlantic Ocean. He had found codfish and trees but no passage to China and no riches that

The Grand Banks, located just off the coast of Newfoundland, supported a thriving fishing industry for over four hundred years. This illustration shows one of the hundreds of schooners from New England that fished on the Grand Banks in the 1800s.

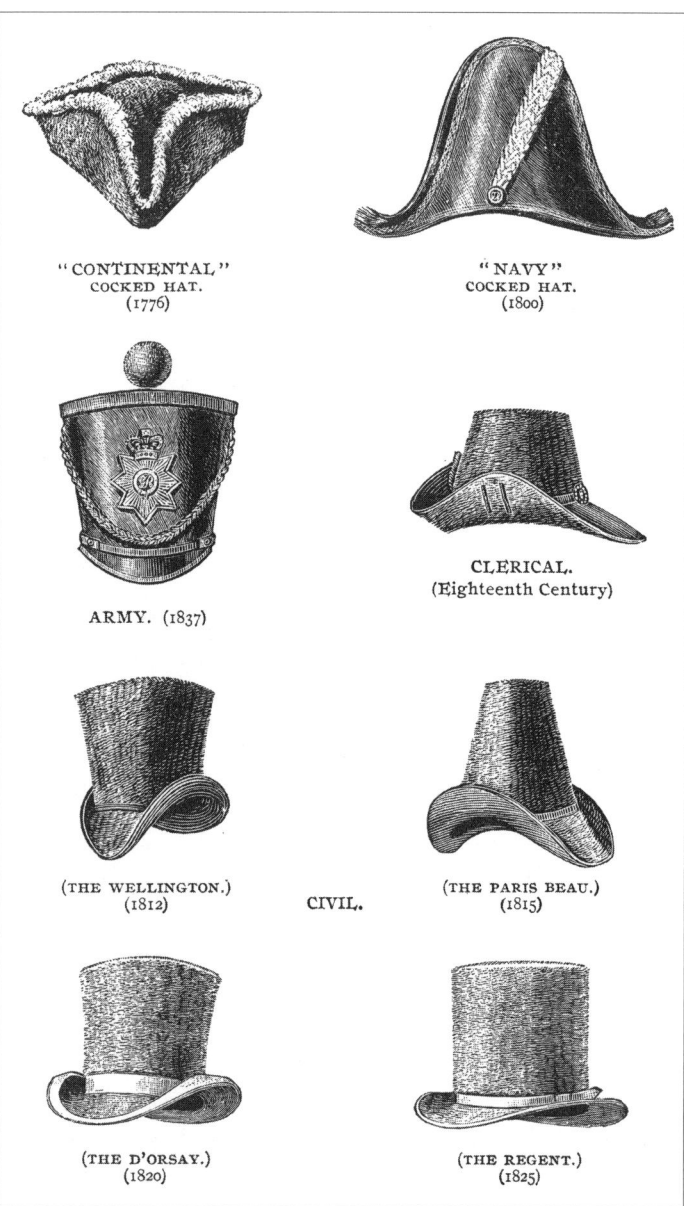

"CONTINENTAL"
COCKED HAT.
(1776)

"NAVY"
COCKED HAT.
(1800)

ARMY. (1837)

CLERICAL.
(Eighteenth Century)

(THE WELLINGTON.)
(1812)

CIVIL.

(THE PARIS BEAU.)
(1815)

(THE D'ORSAY.)
(1820)

(THE REGENT.)
(1825)

At the height of the beaver-hat fashion craze, men wore long curly wigs topped off with huge beaver hats bedecked with feathers. By the 1700s, the good manners of where, when, and how to wear hats were thoroughly embraced by European society.

Why Furs?

So why all the fuss over furs? What made men risk their lives paddling up and down icy rivers and snow-shoeing through endless forests covered in waist-deep snow just to get furs?

It all started with hats—fancy, expensive hats. The fashion fad began way back in the 1500s, and anybody who was somebody in Europe had to have one of these hats. Most of them were made from beaver fur.

In those days, the type of hat you wore symbolized your authority and prestige. The wider the brim of the hat, the more important was its wearer. It's hard to imagine today how important these hats were to European society. No gentleman would ever consider appearing in public without one. The style of his hat indicated his social station, political sympathies, and even his vocation.

A journeyman hatter produced two hats a day in his shop. By the time the workers finished mixing and matting the fur, and shaping, stiffening, and steaming the hat, it was a wonder to behold. Some hats were so stiff that they could support the weight of a two-hundred-pound man. Individual hat shops developed their own recipes for dyes and stiffeners and techniques for waterproofing, which were considered trade secrets. Divulging a secret to a rival shop could be punished by death.

might provide wealth and power for England. It was becoming clear that what Cabot and Columbus before him had found was a new continent that stood between Europe and Asia.

By the first decade of the sixteenth century, word had spread about the fantastic quantities of fish to be found across the Atlantic Ocean. Fishing boats from all over Europe sailed to the Grand Banks. The catches were enormous. With no refrigeration, the piles of fish needed to be preserved, a task usually done onboard ship. Eventually, fishermen from parts of England and the north coast of France began setting up shore stations, where they could dry and salt the fish more easily. There they met Indians of the area who traded furs for goods such as old knives and kettles carried by the fishing vessels.

Fine furs had become a valuable commodity in Europe by the early 1500s and brought a far greater profit than fish did. Fur was more than a luxury: as standards of living rose in the early years of the Renaissance, fur-lined coats, fur collars, fur capes, and muffs became near necessities. The beaver was particularly prized because its glossy fur had an undercoat of short, tightly packed hairs that were perfect for felting. Europe's hatters discovered that when shaved and matted into a stiff felt, beaver fur was the finest hat-making material available. The felt was fashioned into hats of every description.

Fish and furs were fine, but above all, the French and English sought gold, silver, and other riches comparable to what Spanish explorers who followed Columbus had come upon farther south. Spain had laid claim to much of Mexico, Central America, and South America and in the process had discovered a treasure trove of riches. By the mid-1500s, vast silver deposits were uncovered in Mexico, and copper, silver, and gold coins were being milled at the New World's first mint in Mexico City. From New Spain, silver coins called Spanish Dollars became the currency of choice from Europe to Asia, and the Spanish galleons that transported the heavy chests of coins back to Europe became targets for English, French, and Dutch pirates who prowled the Caribbean Sea.

Awareness of the staggering wealth of New Spain to the south convinced the French and English that they could have the same success in the north if they just kept looking. So in 1534, the king of France commissioned an experienced sailor by the name of Jacques Cartier to search for a passage to China either around or through the New World. Cartier was also urged by the king to claim for France all the lands he discovered on his journey. When he arrived in Newfoundland twenty days later, Cartier discovered a barren, uninviting land. "I am rather inclined to believe that this is the land God gave to Cain," he wrote.

Continuing southwest along the coast, he found and charted the Gulf of St. Lawrence, which he thought was just another large bay. He couldn't know that within one hundred years the St. Lawrence would be the artery by which France would control nearly three-quarters of North America.

On July 7, 1534, as Cartier sailed along the coastline of what is now Canada's province of New Brunswick, a fleet of fifty canoes filled with Micmac Indians approached his ship. After some hesitation, Cartier met with the leader of the group. Small items were exchanged in friendship, recorded in Cartier's journal as the first trading action between Europeans and the inhabitants of the New World. But when other canoes began to approach the ship, Cartier wasn't sure of their intent and ordered two cannon shots fired to scare them away.

A few days after that first meeting, forty canoes filled with three hundred Indians from far up the St. Lawrence River approached Cartier's ship "brandishing peltry on sticks—a sure sign that European fishermen had been there before," Cartier wrote in his journal, convinced now that he sailed into territory that had been previously discovered. "We made them signs that we wished them no harm and sent two men ashore to deal with them, bringing knives and other cutlery, and a red cap to give to their chief." The Indians fed the explorers strips of boiled seal meat and, in return for gifts of axes, knives, and rosary beads, they gave all the furs they wore.

Their chief, Donnacona, had led his people down the river with the hope of capturing a part in the growing fur trade with the French explorers and fishermen. They had come from a far-off village named Stadacona. Today, Quebec City, Canada, sits on the land Stadacona's longhouses occupied. But in Cartier's time, the vast region was a wooded wilderness that the explorer intended to claim for France. He planted a towering wooden cross at the edge of the

St. Lawrence bearing the words *Long Live the King of France.*

Chief Donnacona, along with his brother and three of his sons, approached Cartier's ship to protest the claim. While pretending to offer the Indians an ax, the Frenchmen seized the canoe and forced the Indians onto the ship. Cartier reassured them and was able to convince Donnacona to allow two of his sons to return to France with him, promising to bring them back. Accounts differ as to whether the two sons were kidnapped or were allowed by their father to leave with the French. Whatever the circumstance, shortly thereafter Cartier left for France intent on impressing his

Canadian artist C. W. Simpson painted this rendition of Cartier raising the cross on the edge of the Gulf of St. Lawrence.

king with the two young Indians, since he had so far been unsuccessful in finding gold, silver, or China.

When he returned the following spring, Cartier was more determined than ever to discover gold and the opening in the continent that would lead him to Asia. Although Donnacona was overjoyed to have his sons returned, he became suspicious when it was obvious that Cartier intended to keep going up the river past Stadacona to Hochelaga, the home of a larger, more powerful tribe than Donnacona's. If Cartier established ties with this group, it might interfere with Donnacona's plans to act as a middleman in the fur trade.

In his efforts to deter him from Hochelaga to the west, the chief told exaggerated stories of a land to the north named Saguenay—a fabulous place of gold, exotic riches, and white-skinned people who looked like the French. He also warned Cartier that his entire group might die if they attempted to winter away from the protection

This 1850s drawing depicts Jacques Cartier's first meeting in 1535 with the Indians at Hochelaga, the village that became Montreal.

of his village. Undeterred, Cartier set off for Hochelaga and its main village of over two thousand people, located at the site of present-day Montreal. When he finally arrived, he found a farming village, not a vast city of wealth and power he had hoped to discover. The disappointed Cartier returned to Stadacona for the winter.

By Christmas many of his men suffered from scurvy, a mysterious disease that soon killed twenty-five of them. The Stadaconans were also suddenly hit by a deadly disease, perhaps measles or smallpox, and fifty members of the community died. This was possibly the first of a deadly series of European diseases that would eventually sweep through North America, killing more than 75 percent of the Indian population.

When spring finally came, the frustrated and empty-handed Cartier decided to kidnap Donnacona, his two bilingual sons, and several other villagers. He would present them before the king with their stories of the golden city of Saguenay. He hoped these tales, with their spectacular possibilities of gold and other riches, would entice the king to fund yet another voyage.

The next day, Cartier's ship, carrying Donnacona and nine other villagers, departed for France. Wailing Indians in birchbark canoes, bearing beaver and seal pelts as ransom, paddled frantically in the vessel's wake. By the time Cartier sailed a final time to Canada in 1541 with five ships and fifteen hundred men, all of his Indian captives had died in France.

Although Cartier was determined to colonize the new land, the venture quickly ended in failure after he spent a miserable winter fighting off the Indians who hadn't forgotten that he had earlier kidnapped their chief. In June he set out for France with a supply of what he believed was gold and diamonds gathered from the shores of the St. Lawrence River.

The king was ecstatic over this cache of "gold and diamonds." However, the gold turned out to be worthless iron pyrite—fool's gold—and the diamonds were nothing but quartz. With only a pile of rocks to show for France's effort, it seemed that Canada offered little to compensate for the money spent to finance all the expensive voyages. France's plan to colonize Canada was delayed for more than sixty years while the country was preoccupied with problems at home and wars with Spain. The explorers and the king had failed to recognize that the real gold of the New World's wilderness was furs.

Despite Cartier's failure, fishing boats from France continued sailing on their own to the Grand Banks and the New World. By the end of the 1500s, fishing had become secondary as fur trading began in earnest. Indians from the interior paddled their birchbark canoes hundreds of miles on the network of rivers flowing into the St. Lawrence to trade with the French along the huge river's wooded shores. They exchanged mink, ermine, and beaver pelts for metal goods that they brought back to their villages to trade with even more remote tribes. Within just a few years, European merchandise found its way inland nearly fifteen hundred miles.

In less than a century, Columbus, Cabot, and Cartier—one after another—had led a succession of discoveries from islands to fish to furs.

CHAPTER 2

"They Would Offer Us Battle"

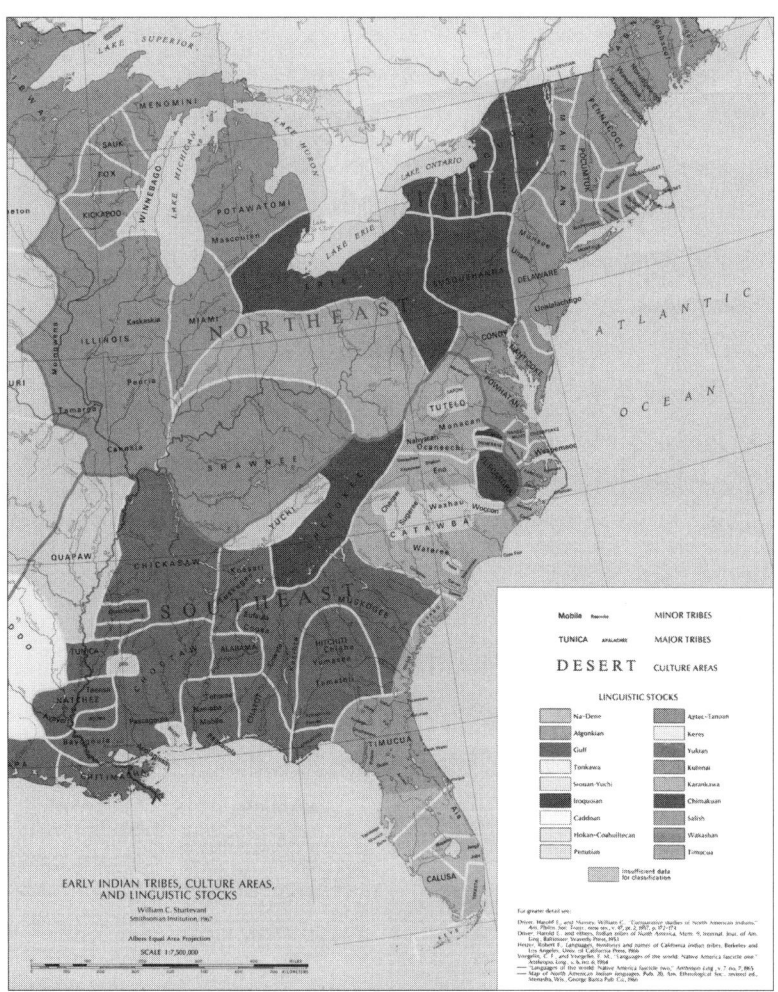

In 1967, well-known anthropologist William C. Sturtevant, curator of North American Ethnology at the National Museum of Natural History of the Smithsonian Institution, created this map of the early Indian tribes, cultural areas, and language boundaries of the eastern half of the United States.

Trade was an ancient, well-organized Indian activity long before Cartier and other Europeans came to North America. Indians understood trade. Farming tribes from the fertile valleys around the Great Lakes traded grain with hunting tribes living farther north. Woodland Indians from the western reaches of the Great Lakes traded forest products to the people of the plains even farther west. Valuable stone, shell, and copper tools traveled thousands of miles through the continent as they were traded among different tribes. The Indians welcomed the opportunity to trade furs with the Europeans for tools and cloth that made their lives more convenient.

Dozens of diverse tribes inhabited the Great Lakes region when the Europeans first arrived. They spoke different languages, and their cultures were as different from one another as today's Swedes are from Spaniards, or Portuguese are from Poles. Some tribes focused on trade, others farmed, while still others hunted, fished, and trapped. The lands they inhabited were not owned in the sense that Europeans recognized land ownership but were understood to be theirs to use. This concept, along with other fundamental differences in the Indians' world view compared with that of the Europeans', would cause problems in the future.

Cartier's attempts at colonizing the newly discovered lands of eastern Canada had failed. But the trade in furs continued. Every summer, French fishermen crossed the Atlantic and often sailed up the St. Lawrence looking for furs. And every summer, Indians from the interior waited for them with piles of furs trapped in their own territories or traded from tribes farther west and north.

As the years passed and the trade expanded, the balance of power along the St. Lawrence began to shift. The Iroquois tribes, which lived in a landlocked region of what is now the state of New York, conducted raids on the Huron tribes to the north in an attempt to seize a piece of the river and its trade. For decades, the Iroquois had fought with their Huron neighbors and with other tribes to the east and west of their home territory.

At one point before Europeans came into the area, the Iroquois had been nearly wiped out by their enemies, only to return within a decade to become even more powerful than ever. Their constant attacks and vicious reputation made them the infamous warring tribes of the region.

The Huron enemies of the Iroquois coined their name, which meant "snake" or "terrifying man." The Five Nations of the Iroquois deserved the reputation. Their League Council maintained harmony among the Mohawk, Oneida, Onondaga, Cayuga, and Seneca tribes so they had the energy and enthusiasm to turn their hostilities against all their neighbors, including the Huron. Skill and valor in war established the status of Iroquois men. Nothing was as important as avenging injuries inflicted on members of their clans.

Into this struggle for power and territory sailed a French explorer named Samuel de Champlain. Having been trained as a painter and draftsman in France, Champlain first traveled to the New World in 1598 on a voyage that took him to the West Indies. In 1603, at the age of thirty-three, he traveled as a passenger

Iroquois leader Etow Oh Koam, called Nicholas by the British, was one of four Mohawk leaders who went to England in 1710. Young and handsome, Nicholas and the other three visitors caused quite a stir in London. Each had his portrait painted by artist John Verelst.

The Five Nations of the Iroquois

For hundreds of years before Samuel de Champlain's arrival in North America, Iroquoian-speaking people had lived around the Lower Great Lakes. They farmed the land and lived in villages of longhouses that contained up to two thousand people. Sometime in the 1500s, they organized themselves into a powerful league or confederacy that consisted of five great Iroquoian tribes: the Mohawk, the Oneida, the Onondaga, the Cayuga, and the Seneca. Although significantly outnumbered by the Huron tribes, the political unity enjoyed by the Five Nations of the Iroquois, as the tribes were called, provided them with many more skilled warriors.

The Five Nations of the Iroquois allowed each member-nation considerable independence but offered crucial alliances for war. One hundred fifty years later, when the American colonies on the Atlantic Coast considered independence from Great Britain, the Five Nations of the Iroquois may have provided a model. In 1744, Iroquois chief Canassatego told a gathering of American commissioners at Lancaster, Pennsylvania, "We heartily recommend Union and a good Agreement between you. … Our wise forefathers established union and amity between the Five Nations. This has made us formidable. This has given us great weight and authority with our neighboring Nations."

The official transcripts of that meeting were hand delivered to newspaper publisher Benjamin Franklin in Philadelphia. He printed the proceedings in his paper, the *Philadelphia Gazette*. Many historians believe Canassatego's ideas planted a seed in Franklin's mind and in the minds of those who read his paper when they eventually confronted the fate of the British colonies.

on a fur trading ship, sailing the region around the St. Lawrence River that many were beginning to call New France. The details in his journals and accounts of his expeditions illustrate that Champlain was an adventurer and a meticulous mapmaker. Eager to see and know everything, he had a curiosity and an enthusiasm that were unbounded. Champlain drew a map of the coastline, wrote detailed descriptions of new tribes he encountered, searched for gold mines, and shot river rapids in a birchbark canoe.

Samuel de Champlain, who first arrived in New France in 1603, is considered the founding father of Canada.

In late May 1603, he and his fellow passengers witnessed the Huron tribe's spring feast, which included dancing and foot races. While the rest of the crew traded for furs, Champlain noted in his journal that he had time to study the Huron customs and to give some of the Indians a lesson in religion.

But what lay to the west continued to attract Champlain. He believed, like Cabot and Cartier before him, that the Asian Sea to China was not far away. By questioning the Huron, he was able to draw a remarkably accurate map of the Great Lakes, including Niagara Falls, an area no European had yet seen. Determined to follow the St. Lawrence until he found the Northwest Passage that would take him through the continent, Champlain sailed upstream as soon as the trading ended. His group was stopped by the extensive river rapids at Hochelaga, the village visited by Cartier nearly seventy years before.

The French king had granted royal charters, or permits, to explorers like Champlain, allowing them to trade within the huge area of New France on the condition that they start a colony there—never mind that the land was already occupied by dozens of Indian tribes. Since it was accepted that the king had control over the people, the trade, and the exploration of everything within his realm, he granted permission to those he supported to carry out his work.

In 1608, Champlain and twenty-seven other men once again paddled upstream to the site of today's Quebec City, Donnacona's hometown of Stadacona. The remnants of Donnacona's tribe had long since abandoned the area and moved farther

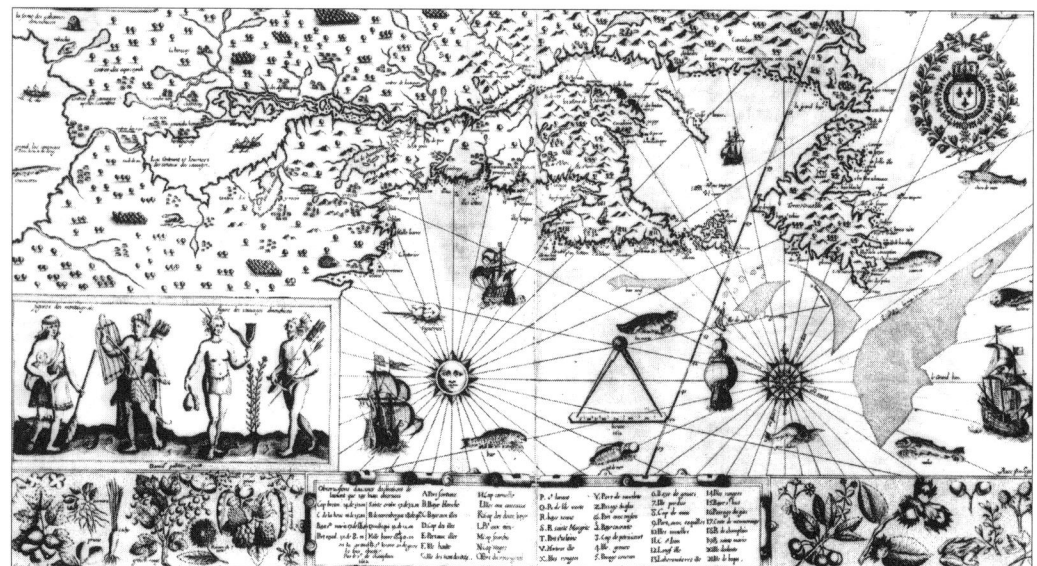

Samuel de Champlain's 1612 map of New France illustrates the eastern region of what is now the Maritime Provinces of Canada and is decorated with drawings of the area's plants and animals as well as scenes of Indian life.

New France

New France was founded in 1608 by Samuel de Champlain when he and twenty-eight men settled at Quebec. Although sponsored by Henry IV of France, colonization was long and hard because of the weather and diseases such as scurvy that plagued the settlers. By 1627, only one hundred colonists lived in the settlement.

That year, Cardinal Richelieu, adviser to King Louis XIII, founded the Company of One Hundred Associates to invest in New France in an attempt to make it as populous and wealthy as the English colonies to the south. He promised land parcels called seigneuries to Catholic colonists who agreed to settle the land and work to make it an important trading and farming colony. Initially, few Frenchmen took him up on the offer. The thickly wooded land coupled with brutal winters far more severe than those of France made the prospect of colonization discouraging.

The Catholic Church was powerful in New France, which by 1700 stretched from the St. Lawrence River through the Great Lakes region and south along the Mississippi River. The colony was governed by a series of leaders appointed by the French king. They were responsible for ensuring the expansion of French territory and trading interests in North America. The struggle with Great Britain and the Iroquois Indians to the south for power, wealth, and territory continued until New France fell to the British at the end of the French and Indian War in 1763.

west. As the frigid fall winds blew in from the north, Champlain and his group built a tiny log outpost and settled in for the winter.

Winters in the St. Lawrence Valley four hundred years ago were colder, snowier, and far more brutal than they are now. The world was in the midst of a period called the Little Ice Age, which began about 1350 and lasted for nearly five hundred years. Snows piled up four to five feet deep, and the rivers and lakes remained frozen far into the spring. Champlain's men struggled with the bitter cold.

By spring, twenty of Champlain's men were dead from scurvy or dysentery. But instead of turning back, Champlain pushed on upstream with his bedraggled winterers. Within a few days, the handful of survivors came upon a group of Huron Indians who were on their way to attack their Iroquois enemies to the south. The Huron asked for Champlain's help. Recognizing an opportunity to expand his "territory" and influence, he readily agreed. Champlain and two of his men joined the war party.

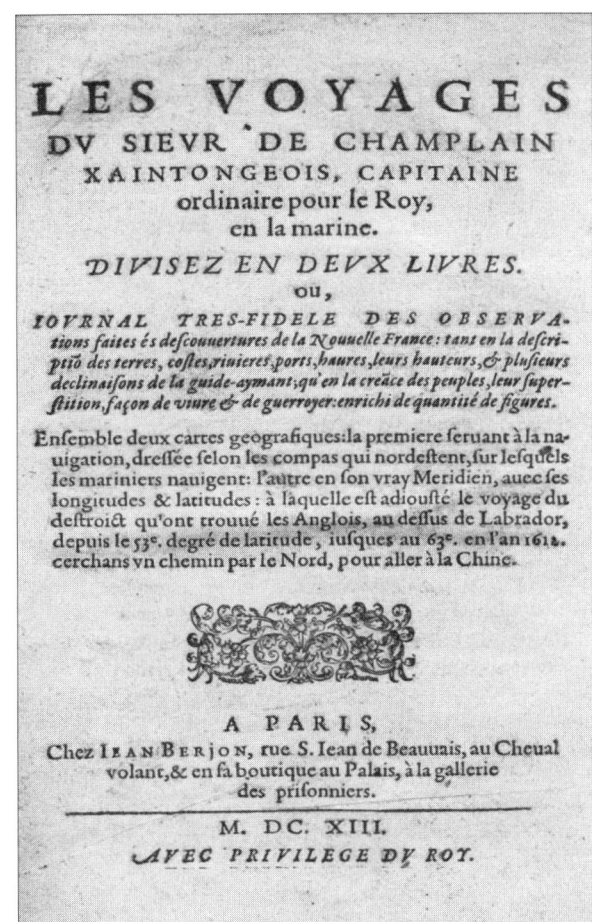

This is the title page of one of Samuel de Champlain's journals that describes his adventures in New France.

Champlain's journal of 1609 vividly recalls what took place on this trip south into Iroquois country. He sat toward the front of a huge birchbark canoe, his long, flowing hair covered by a wide-brimmed felt hat. Paintings of him from the time show a dark mustache and narrow, trimmed beard on a chin that tilted at a regal, almost arrogant angle. He carefully surveyed the new countryside and likely thought about how this bountiful land could fit into his plans for expanding French access south of his tiny settlement at Quebec. He would claim the land for France, and he would trade for furs directly from the Indians. The future looked bright.

The Huron who paddled the twenty-four birchbark canoes came from the rolling hills and fertile valleys north of Lake Ontario and were mortal enemies of the Iroquois to the south. Their goal was to attack and push the Iroquois still farther south, and with Champlain's help they felt assured of success.

As they moved along the river, Champlain noted the abundance of beavers in the area and the thick stands of pine and chestnut trees. The river and shoreline teemed with other fur-bearing animals, such as bear and deer.

As the shallow stream widened into a huge lake that would eventually be named after him, Champlain squinted into the warm morning sunlight. At a distance off to his left, the Green Mountains rose against the sun, a few patches of snow still clinging to their tops. On the right and to the south, another forested range of mountains known as the Adirondacks stretched out along the horizon. The lake's clear, deep water magnified the huge fish, "which were as large as my thigh," Champlain wrote, "the head being as big as my two fists, with a snout two feet and a half long, and a double row of very sharp and dangerous teeth. ..."

This lithograph from a history book published in 1893 shows Samuel de Champlain and two companions exploring the Canadian wilderness accompanied by Indians who are portaging the group's canoes.

Aided by descriptions given him by the Huron, Champlain estimated the lake was nearly three hundred miles long. It contained four large islands that had formerly been inhabited by the Iroquois but now stood empty because the area was a war zone. Battles between the Huron and the Iroquois had been raging here for decades.

The Huron explained that the mountains ahead were densely settled with Iroquois. The powerful Iroquois nation inhabited much of the region around the huge lake and the mountains beyond.

Champlain and his group paddled farther into

enemy territory, traveling only at night to avoid detection. Just after dusk on the evening of July 29, 1609, the war party once again launched their canoes. The high-pitched whistles and low, echoing croaks of thousands of tree toads and frogs muffled the sounds of the paddlers as they made their way a few hundred yards from shore. Each man scanned the glassy water and dark silhouette of the shoreline for the enemy. At about ten o'clock, as the war party reached the tip of Crown Point on the western shore of the lake, silvery ripples on the water revealed a flotilla of heavy oak canoes paddled by what Champlain guessed were nearly two hundred Iroquois warriors.

Each party saw the other. "We both began to utter loud cries," Champlain wrote, "all getting their arms in readiness." Being closest to shore, the Iroquois landed and, for several hours in pitch-black darkness, feverishly hacked down trees and brush to create a barricade. Champlain and the Huron lashed their canoes together with poles and watched the battle preparation as they floated a mere bowshot away.

When the Iroquois completed the barricade and were armed and ready, they pushed off two canoes from the shore. Representatives paddled to the Huron "to inquire if they wished to fight, to which the latter replied that they wanted nothing else," Champlain wrote. "But [the Iroquois] said that, at present, there was not much light, and that it would be necessary to wait for daylight, so as to be able to recognize each other; and that, as soon as the sun rose, they would offer us battle."

The harquebus was a primitive hand-held firearm that reached its peak of popularity in the early 1500s. The shooter could hold the gun with both hands, thereby getting a better aim at his target.

After this incredible exchange, which Champlain witnessed from his hiding place under a blanket at the bottom of a canoe, "the entire night was spent dancing and singing, on both sides, with endless insults and other talk." The Iroquois warned the Huron that the early morning light would see their demise. The floating warriors hurled back similar threats.

At dawn, after strapping on metal breastplates and plumed helmets, the three Frenchmen hid in separate canoes. Each held his heavy French musket, an old, outdated firearm called a harquebus. Champlain's was loaded with four lead balls.

As the Huron paddled the short distance to shore, they told Champlain that the enemies who wore three large feathers were the chiefs, and Champlain should do what he could to kill them. When they landed, the warriors ran toward the enemy. Champlain kept to the rear of the group while his two countrymen slipped off into the woods with several Huron. The Iroquois held their ground, ready to attack. Finally, Champlain recalled, "They came at a slow pace towards us, with a dignity and assurance … having three chiefs at their head."

With shouts to Champlain, the Huron warriors opened their ranks so that he could pass to the front of the battle. The astonished Iroquois gaped at him in silence. They had never seen a white man before, much less one with gleaming metal on his chest and head. Champlain marched some twenty paces in front of the rest and stopped

This sketch, drawn by Samuel de Champlain, depicts the battle with the Iroquois on the shore of what is now called Lake Champlain. Champlain is front and center, firing his harquebus. His two companions can be seen firing from the woods above him.

within fifty feet of the enemy, the early morning sunlight glinting from his helmet.

A long moment passed as the Iroquois recovered from their shock. Then when he saw them make a move to attack, Champlain rested his musket against his shoulder and aimed directly at one of the three chiefs. With a single, thunderous shot that echoed across the water, two Iroquois chiefs fell to the ground dead, and a third warrior lay badly wounded.

There arose such a yell from the attackers, Champlain recalled, that it would have drowned a thunderclap. A shower of arrows rained from both sides. As Champlain reloaded his weapon, another deafening gunshot exploded from the thick brush where his two companions hid, "which astonished them anew to such a degree," Champlain wrote, "that, seeing their chiefs dead, they lost courage and took to flight, abandoning their camp and fort, and fleeing into the woods, whither I pursued them, killing still more of them." With their leaders lying dead from the mysterious new weapon, the shocked Iroquois warriors fled in terror.

The old French guns had scared off the mighty Iroquois. The Huron were ecstatic, and Champlain was all but adopted by the northern Indians.

His growing respect for the Huron's knowledge of the vast North American lands and their skill at navigating the rivers and rapids of the interior helped him recognize that the key to French success in the New World was held by his newfound friends. In the years that followed, Champlain encouraged his men to use birchbark canoes, learn the Indian languages, and adopt many skills of the native woodsmen.

Champlain had no idea that his skirmish with the Iroquois had created an enemy whose future alliance with the British would lead to New France's eventual demise. The battle on Lake Champlain in the summer of 1609 set the scene for more fur trade and two centuries of trouble.

CHAPTER 3

"They Attack Like Lions"

Canadian historical illustrator and landscape painter C. W. Jefferys drew this sketch, Étienne Brûlé at the Mouth of the Humber. Jefferys sought to bring Canadian history to life by filling his art with defining moments of the country's past.

Champlain's friendship with the Huron tribes grew after the victory over the Iroquois. The warriors agreed to take one of his men, twenty-three-year-old Étienne Brûlé, to their home in the densely settled region of rolling hills and fertile valleys between Lakes Huron and Ontario. There Brûlé would learn their language and encourage trade to the west. He traveled with the Indians on winding rivers and what appeared to be vast inland seas all the way to Lake Superior, the largest freshwater lake in the world. When he returned to Quebec, he reported that there was an incredible abundance of furs to be found farther west.

The stories Brûlé told helped Champlain begin to imagine the opportunities available in the wilderness. His men adopted the Indians' clothing, snowshoes, and moccasins, learned their languages, and began using the birchbark canoe as their primary mode of river transportation.

By the time Champlain died of a stroke in Quebec on Christmas Day, 1635, he had crossed the Atlantic Ocean twenty-three times—an amazing accomplishment even by today's standards. He had spent thirteen winters in Canada and had repeatedly risked his life to explore the vast territories of New France. His ear had been split by an Iroquois arrow that lodged in his neck. He had nearly drowned several times while learning to handle a birchbark canoe. He had mapped most of New France and had built the beginnings of Quebec. His original dream of finding the Northwest Passage to the riches of China had been eclipsed by the quest for furs, North America's "soft gold."

The traders that followed Champlain developed wilderness knowledge and trading expertise that was envied by the Dutch and English who were attempting to trade for furs south of New France. Over time, through hand gestures and trial and error, nearly every French trader learned the Indian languages and attempted to adapt to the cultural traditions of the various tribes.

Trading sessions always began with gift-giving and often included the ritual of smoking a peace pipe. Then the trade goods such as kettles, axheads, cloth, and knives were exchanged for beaver pelts. In most cases, no money changed hands. The beaver was the unit of currency. The prices of all the trader's goods were figured according to the value equal to one good beaver skin. Even the hunter's labor was counted in beavers, not in hours.

As trade expanded throughout the rivers and lakes that drained into the St. Lawrence Valley of New France, it also spread westward from the Atlantic seaboard. When an English religious group called the Pilgrims decided to sail to the New World in 1620, they settled in Massachusetts. The Pilgrims purchased their lands from the Plymouth Company in England with the pledge of an annual payment of otter, moose, and beaver furs. The Plymouth Company had been granted an English royal charter to found colonial

The 1804 ledger from the fur post on the Snake River in Minnesota tallies trade goods in terms of beaver skins.

"Soft Gold"

Beaver fur was sometimes called soft gold. By the mid-1600s, beaver and other furs shipped from the New World were worth more than money. The hats made from it eventually became so valuable that they were left as bequests in wills.

In 1641, Governor Thomas Mayhew, a successful Massachusetts merchant, purchased several islands off the coast of Cape Cod, including Martha's Vineyard, Nantucket, and the Elizabeth Islands. He must have really wanted a beaver hat because some years later it is recorded that he sold the island of Nantucket for thirty pounds sterling and two beaver hats, one for himself and one for his wife.

TOP *Galleons similar to this model ship carried silver, gold, and other treasures from the Spanish colonies in the New World to Spain. Fleets of up to fifty ships sailed across the Atlantic Ocean and then returned with manufactured goods for the colonies.*

ABOVE *This early French depiction of an Iroquois warrior shows him wearing snowshoes and carrying a gun, a sword, wampum beads, and a fierce scowl on his tattooed face.*

settlements along the eastern coast of North America. In addition to those annual payments of furs, the colonists needed something they could sell in England in exchange for the manufactured goods they needed. Furs became their cash crop.

At about the same time, a trading firm called the Dutch West India Company began developing the fur trade and settlements along the Hudson, Delaware, and Connecticut rivers south of Champlain's New France. Founded in 1621 by a group of Dutch merchants, the trading company was granted exclusive trading rights to the area—called a monopoly—by the Dutch government. The company focused on establishing trade on the Atlantic seaboard and expended great energy and enthusiasm intercepting silver-ladened Spanish ships on their way from Mexico to Spain.

More Dutch people settled at the southern tip of the island of Manhattan, now New York City, and farther south, English colonists settled in Virginia. While they were busy clearing land and building, the colonists in all areas needed trappers to supply them with furs. The Iroquois tribes gladly accommodated them, and as the new settlements grew and prospered, both the Indian trappers and English and Dutch colonists profited. By 1630, the Iroquois had acquired guns from the Dutch through this trade and had pretty well depleted the supply of beavers in the Hudson River valley of New York.

With guns in hand and an eye on a much larger and more lucrative trading network to the north, the Iroquois launched a brutal and successful war against the Huron and the French in New France. Within ten years, the attackers had encircled the St. Lawrence River region and pushed the Huron Indians, along with many other Algonquin-speaking tribes, north and west. The French colonial government and traders were forced to spend great amounts of time and money trying to defend themselves against the invaders, who effectively blockaded all of the fur trade in New France.

The Iroquois were ferocious warriors. A Jesuit priest wrote that "in their method of warfare the Iroquois are so stealthy in their approach, so swift in their execution. ... They come

In the 1640s and 1650s, none of the French colonists of the St. Lawrence Valley felt safe from hostile Iroquois attacks. This woodcut illustration shows Iroquois warriors lurking near a French settlement.

like foxes through the woods. ... They attack like lions, and, as their surprises are made when they are least expected, they meet with no resistance. They take flight like birds, disappearing before they have really appeared."

Between 1646 and 1648, nearly half the Huron people died from violent Iroquois invasions and the ravages of European diseases like smallpox and measles from which they had no immunity. Hundreds more died of starvation when their stores of food were burned in the wake of the attacks. The war all but shut down the fur trade in North America.

Back in Europe, constant wars in Spain and England so preoccupied the French government that it offered little assistance to the struggling little colony of New France. If the far-flung forts along the St. Lawrence and its tributaries were to survive, the funds had to come from the fur trade. And the only people who could succeed in the trade during the Iroquois blockade were those who knew the land

New France's regulated trade nearly disappeared in the mid-1600s when the French coureur des bois, *or woods runners, used their well-honed skills in wilderness survival and trading with the Indians to bypass all the government rules.*

as well as the Indians did and could live and survive in the north woods for months or even years.

A group of young traders who had learned the ways of the wilderness from the Indians became the lifeline of the fur trade. Known as woods runners, most were born in New France and often spent their summers clearing and trying to farm the land along the St. Lawrence. In the fall they traveled inland to the Huron or Ojibwa camps, where they spent the winter trading. When the rivers cleared of ice in the spring, they smuggled their furs through the Iroquois line to Quebec.

Most of the woods runners could neither read nor write and were of such a low social rank that they could not obtain trading licenses from the French colonial government, which favored people who had wealth, education, and connections to the crown. The licenses required fees to be paid to the government along with a percentage of the traders' profits. The woods runners ignored the rules and the licenses, left the farmland their government wanted them to work, and sought their fortunes in the wilderness. The unlicensed, illegal trade began to flourish because no one else had the survival skills or the Indian-language skills to be successful.

One of these woods runners left France in his late teens and arrived in New France in 1641. His name was Medard Seigneur Chouart des Groseilliers, whose name in French means "gooseberries." Better educated than most, he initially found work with the Jesuit missionaries in the area around Lake Huron. A sad-eyed, mustached adventurer and a natural leader, Groseilliers learned the Indian languages at the mission

Father Jacques Marquette, a Jesuit missionary, descended the Mississippi River in 1673.

Evangelizing the Indians

Although exploration and colonization were primary goals of the French adventurers who penetrated the St. Lawrence Valley, they brought with them Catholic missionaries who were committed to converting the Indians to Christianity.

By the time Cardinal Richelieu, adviser to King Louis XIII, named Samuel de Champlain governor of New France in 1627, Jesuit missionaries had penetrated the Great Lakes region and converted many of the Indians. The priests were usually young men who took vows to live in poverty and serve God by helping others. Called Black Robes by the Indians, they learned the native languages and used this skill to keep peace between the tribes.

Father Jacques Marquette and Father Louis Hennepin are two of the many missionaries who traveled with French explorers into the interior of North America.

but was driven back to Quebec by the war with the Iroquois.

When the Iroquois finally signed a peace treaty with the French in 1653, the blockade around the St. Lawrence River was lifted. A group of Huron Indians who had fled all the way to present-day Wisconsin during the war returned to Quebec to trade. When they started west again in August, Groseilliers went with them. Over the next two years, he traveled all over Wisconsin and Michigan, trading and mapping the area. In the spring of 1656, Groseilliers returned to Quebec with fifty canoes filled with a fortune in furs.

The French colonial authorities in Quebec were furious. Groseilliers didn't hold a license to trade, and independent trading didn't add desperately needed money to the government's treasury. When Groseilliers tried to purchase a trading license, the governor demanded half the fur-trading profits. When the trader refused, he was forbidden to leave New France. Unfazed

Pierre-Esprit Radisson, sketched here by an unknown artist, arrived in New France in 1651. In his journals, he describes in detail his trading adventures in the western Great Lakes region and his later involvement with the Hudson's Bay Company in Upper Canada.

by the official grounding, Groseilliers immediately teamed up with his young brother-in-law, Pierre Esprit Radisson, slipped past the authorities, and once again paddled west.

Radisson's knowledge of the Indians and their ways had been acquired more painfully than Groseilliers's. At the age of fifteen, while duck hunting on a lake in northern New York, he was kidnapped by a band of Iroquois warriors who took him to their village on what is now known as Lake Champlain. He was adopted by an Iroquois family and spent the next five years participating in war-party raids of enemy tribes and becoming, in effect, a white Indian. When he crushed the skulls of three Iroquois warriors in a middle-of-the-night attempt to escape back to New France, he was recaptured and tortured. Two years later, he successfully escaped and returned to Quebec. Radisson's deep knowledge of Indian culture, gained from his years with the Iroquois, would serve him well.

Groseilliers and Radisson became so close that they often referred to each other as brothers. They paddled as far west as Lake Superior on the route that thousands of fur traders would take in the coming years. During their trip, they heard stories from the Indians of "a great store of beaver" near the Hudson Bay to the north. They were told the bay was only a week's canoe journey from the eastern shore of Lake Superior, and there the beaver pelts were the glossiest and finest anywhere.

When they returned this time to Quebec, they had sixty birchbark canoes loaded with beaver pelts, and they had a great idea. New France could establish trading posts on Hudson Bay and avoid the Iroquois attacks in the south that continued despite the earlier peace treaty. The master woods runners anticipated huge success with their brilliant plan.

But as soon as their brigade of fur-packed canoes touched the riverbank at Quebec, New France's colonial governor, the Marquis d'Argenson, seized the entire illegal treasure for the government and briefly threw Groseilliers into jail for again trading without a license.

The confiscated furs from this western trip are credited with saving the colony from economic ruin, but their loss so angered Radisson and Groseilliers that they decided to seek support for their Hudson Bay plan elsewhere. Radisson wrote in his journal: "He made my brother prisoner for not having obeyed his orders. ... Seeing ourselves so wronged, my brother did resolve to go and demand justice in France."

After an unsuccessful trip to France to resolve their mistreatment, the two traveled to Boston, which was a thriving colonial city at the time. For the next three years, Groseilliers and Radisson tried to persuade traders there to sponsor voyages to Hudson Bay. Finally, with help from a commissioner sent by Charles II, they sailed for England. Dressed as Indian fur traders in deerskin leggings and moccasins, they appeared before the king. They told exaggerated stories of life in the wilderness and of the bountiful fur trade around Hudson Bay.

Charles II, known as the "merry monarch," had been restored to the throne in 1660 after the bleak ten-year rule of Oliver Cromwell. Cromwell and his Puritan followers had attempted to run England as a republic ruled by the people instead of by a king or queen. But the experiment ended in failure. During the religiously strict era of Cromwell, theaters shut down, stained-glass church windows were smashed for their gaudiness, and even the most innocent of amusements such as dancing around a flower-decked maypole were banned. It was considered illegal to

The Last Voyage of Henry Hudson *by John Collier shows the explorer adrift in the Arctic with his son after a mutiny by Hudson's crew in 1611.*

Henry Hudson

In 1609, Henry Hudson, an English navigator and explorer, initially attempted to discover a *northeast* passage to China around the top of Russia. But when ice blocked his way, he turned west, sailed across the Atlantic, and ended up exploring New York Harbor and the river that flowed into it from the north that now bears his name. He sailed north all the way to what is today Albany, New York, claiming the lands for the Dutch. When the river narrowed and he was forced to turn back, he knew this wasn't the passage to China he was seeking.

In 1610, he once again set sail west. In early August of that year, he discovered a huge bay that he was confident was the Northwest Passage. After spending months exploring, he and his crew were forced to winter on the shore of the bay. In the spring of 1611 when the weather warmed, Hudson readied to enthusiastically continue his explorations. His crew, however, had other ideas. In June they mutinied and placed Hudson, his teenage son, and seven crewmen loyal to him in a small boat with no food or water. The rebellious crew set sail for England, and Hudson was never seen again.

FAR LEFT In 1666, King Charles II was dazzled by Radisson and Groseilliers's descriptions of riches to be had in the New World's north woods. Although he was sometimes considered indecisive, the king jumped at the chance to help the fur traders by introducing them to Prince Rupert.

LEFT Prince Rupert, Charles II's cousin, stood 6 feet 4 inches tall and was an influential presence at the English court. In 1670, he became the first governor of the Hudson's Bay Company and the 1.5 million square miles of Canada that it controlled.

go walking on Sundays except to a religious service. Although Cromwell had replaced King Charles II, who thought he had absolute powers, the strict, controlling "republic" proved to be even worse.

When Charles II finally was reinstated as king, the people were so happy with the return of freedom that it spawned creativity in all areas of English life. The biggest economic change was a renewed enthusiasm by the government for granting royal charters to overseas trading companies.

Charles loved money and could never get enough of it—what with lavish palaces to maintain and the Royal Navy to equip. So when he met with Radisson and Groseilliers on October 25, 1666, he recognized in the visitors' amazing descriptions a new pattern in fur trading that might be developed for England's benefit. And Radisson's declaration that he had traveled a river that discharged "North West into the South Seas" opened the possibility that going to Hudson Bay might provide piles of rich furs and—even better—offer easy entry to the long-sought Northwest Passage. The expensive journeys to China could be dramatically shortened.

After their success at court, Radisson and Groseilliers were introduced to the king's wealthy cousin, Prince Rupert, who had earned distinction in England as a cavalry leader, king's admiral, pirate, chemist, an inventor, and an entrepreneur.

He knew of the sprawling bay discovered by explorer Henry Hudson several decades earlier and decided to organize a private company to finance an exploratory journey to the bay.

Two ships, the *Eaglet* and the *Nonsuch*, were outfitted and made ready to sail. On the cool, foggy morning of June 3, 1668, Rupert and the other company owners rowed down the Thames River to see the ships off. Groseilliers would sail on the *Nonsuch* and Radisson on the *Eaglet*. But the *Eaglet* was forced to turn back during a storm off Ireland, and only the *Nonsuch* made the voyage. In mid-July, under clouds of squawking seabirds, the little ship sailed into Hudson Strait and ended up wintering in Hudson Bay.

Wintering in the far north was not a problem for Groseilliers, who had years of experience in the wilderness. He supervised the preparations for the frigid months to come. The *Nonsuch* was hauled up on the shore, and then the men chopped down dozens of pine trees to create a clearing. A stockade of vertical logs was set around a small log house chinked with moss and roofed with thatch gathered from a nearby swamp.

The crew spent the winter eating netted fish and wild geese, and when spring finally arrived, a group of three hundred James Bay

When French explorer Jean Nicolet waded ashore at Green Bay in 1634, he was welcomed by the Winnebago Indians, who inhabited a large part of eastern Wisconsin. Today, ancestors of the Winnebagos, known as the Ho-Chunk Nation, still reside in the area.

Still Searching for the Northwest Passage

In the seventeenth century, even with mounting geographical evidence to the contrary, many people still thought it was possible to reach China overland from New France or the English colonies. In 1633, Samuel de Champlain sent the French explorer Jean Nicolet into the western Great Lakes region, where he discovered Lake Michigan. Nicolet spent nearly ten years tramping through the north woods with a robe of Chinese silk carefully folded in his pack so that when he met Chinese officials he would be properly dressed. When he finally donned the dazzling robe at Green Bay, the sight of it terrified the gathered Winnebago Indians. They dropped their weapons and immediately agreed to a peace treaty with the French.

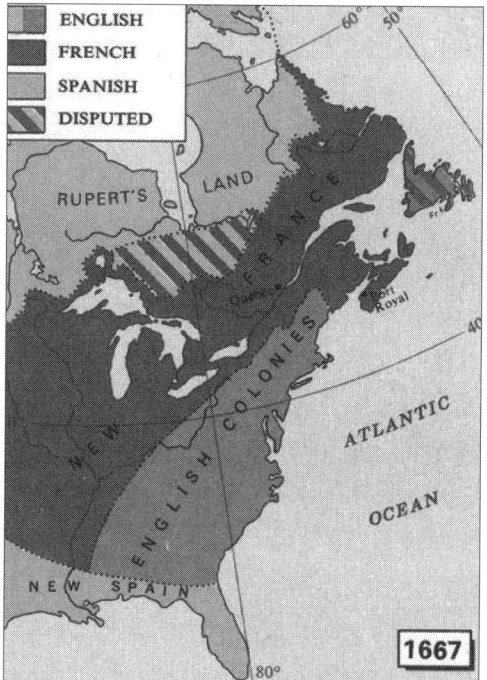

LEFT The Nonsuch *was acquired by Prince Rupert's group in March 1668 for 290 pounds. The sturdy little vessel anchored in James Bay off the mouth of the Rupert River on September 29, 1668—the very same place where Henry Hudson had wintered more than half a century earlier.*

BELOW A map of the eastern half of North America in 1667 shows the English colonies, New France, a portion of New Spain, and the holdings granted to the Hudson's Bay Company by Charles II, called Rupert's Land.

Indians came to trade. Groseilliers supervised the trading of guns, axes, scrapers, needles, and beads for the finest coat beaver. Coat beaver was the fur the Indians wore as clothing and was highly prized because only the thick undercoat of the pelt was present. With the guard hairs of the fur worn off, the part used for hat making was easier to harvest.

The *Nonsuch* returned to England bursting with furs. The success prompted King Charles to present Prince Rupert and his company with the largest land grant the world had known. With Rupert controlling the operations from London, the Hudson's Bay Company claimed vast territory that included the entire Hudson Bay drainage system and parts of what would become the United States. It was called Rupert's Land.

CHAPTER 4

"By Virtue of His Majesty's Commission"

By the time Prince Rupert organized the Hudson's Bay Company, the French fur trade extended around the Great Lakes and beyond. In 1672, an ambitious, overbearing soldier by the name of Louis de Buade de Frontenac was sent by the French king to build forts in New France. Concerned that too much effort was going into fur trading, the king wanted Frontenac, as governor of the colony, to focus on developing farming and perhaps mining. The fur trade was blamed for luring too many able-bodied workers into the woods and weakening the economic and military strength of the colony. Farming and trades like barrel making and blacksmithing were easier to tax and oversee.

This bronze statue of Louis de Buade de Frontenac was created in 1890 by Louis-Philippe Hébert and stands in Quebec City.

Frontenac had distinguished himself for many years as a soldier in France. With his oversized felt hat, elegant uniform, and often scowling face, he cut quite a figure in the colony. He was known for his snappish temper and high opinion of himself. He never really obeyed his orders from France and fought with local church leaders soon after he arrived.

The new governor was determined to do more than just help his struggling colony hunker down and grow more crops. Frontenac's eye was focused on the English fur trade to the south, which by this time had developed into a threatening competitor. Instead of building forts close to the St. Lawrence for the defense of the little farming communities, he forced the residents of Montreal to provide labor and materials to construct a fur-trading post on the eastern edge of Lake Ontario—a long way from where he was supposed to build forts. This annoyed the local colonists and

In 1673, Governor Louis de Buade de Frontenac, depicted here in a watercolor by John Henry de Rinzy, established a fort at the base of Lake Ontario where eventually Kingston, Ontario, would grow.

infuriated the Iroquois, who considered the region their hunting territory.

Frontenac's new fort at the tip of Lake Ontario, which he named after himself, was intended as a base for eventual attacks on the English in the Iroquois country to the south. If successful, New France would have the pesky Iroquois under its control and could stop the steady flow of furs into English territory. Fort Frontenac, located at present-day Kingston, Ontario, became the first in a network of fur-trading stations that the governor built on the Great Lakes and along the tributaries of the Mississippi River.

The English fur trade was centered at Albany, New York, and the Iroquois were strongly allied with those traders. The English colonists paid more for beaver pelts because their trade with England was free from the heavy taxes the French colonists were required to pay when they shipped their furs. And the Iroquois much preferred the goods they acquired from Albany. They particularly liked English guns and the "strouds"—coarse woolen garments that were warmer, fit better, and lasted longer than those made by the French.

Steady French expansion caused more and more friction with the Iroquois tribes and with the woods runners, the independent fur traders who felt the government was interfering with their business. Along with the new forts, Jesuit missions were built. From those outposts, Catholic missionaries worked to convert more Indians to Christianity.

The church, led by the bishop of Quebec, became a powerful force in New France, much to the irritation of Frontenac. The governor's focus was on expanding his colony's fur trading empire, not converting the Indians. So when he issued licenses permitting the trading of brandy and other liquor, the church protested and even sent an ambassador to France to plead for royal enforcement. But despite the loud opposition from both the missionaries and local government officials, Frontenac successfully introduced brandy as a stock Indian trading item.

Less than a year after his arrival in Canada, Frontenac hired Louis Joliet, the son of a wagonmaker from Quebec, to explore farther west than any European had before. Joliet was accompanied by Father Jacques Marquette, a Jesuit priest who spoke several Indian languages. In the spring of 1673, the pair set out with

TOP Father Jacques Marquette and Louis Joliet traveled more than four thousand miles into the North American interior. This print by A. Russell shows them descending the Mississippi River in birchbark canoes.

ABOVE A mural by painter Cal Peters depicts Marquette and Joliet's expedition entering the Mississippi River on June 17, 1673. It is on display at Villa Louis Historic Site, Prairie du Chien, Wisconsin.

two birchbark canoes and five other explorers. They followed Lake Michigan to Green Bay and then up the Fox River of Wisconsin to Lake Winnebago. From there, with the help of two local Indians, they carried, or portaged, their canoes and supplies to the Wisconsin River and followed that southwest. On June 17, they entered the Mississippi River near what is now Prairie du Chien, Wisconsin, becoming the first Europeans to do so.

Joliet and Marquette's expedition paddled to within five hundred miles of the Gulf of Mexico. On the way they met several tribes of Indians and at one point were given a peace pipe by one of the chiefs. When they reached the Arkansas River, Indians with guns suddenly surrounded them. Only the sight of the peace pipe kept the group from attacking.

The Indians told Marquette that their guns had come from other white men who were based about a ten-day journey south. He was also told that the Mississippi flowed into the Gulf of Mexico. Fearing that they might stumble upon explorers or colonists from Spain, France's enemy, Marquette and Joliet decided to turn back.

The dream of René-Robert Cavelier, Sieur de La Salle, was to build a colony for trading at the mouth of the Mississippi River. Instead, he and his colonists landed on the coast of Texas, where they began a doomed journey.

When they returned to Quebec, their report to Frontenac included descriptions of the huge river that flowed through a much warmer area and into the Gulf of Mexico. No ice-bound rivers or waist-deep snow would cause delays in the movement of furs and trade goods there. The Mississippi route might be used year-round.

Just as Joliet and Marquette returned from their two-and-a-half-year exploration of the Mississippi, another explorer set out to expand New France's territorial holdings. He was a young, hotheaded seminary dropout by the name of René-Robert Cavelier, Sieur de La Salle, who was obsessed with the idea of finding a passage to China.

Years earlier, in 1666, La Salle was close to destitute when he sailed to Canada, where his brother, Jean, was a priest in Montreal. Upon La Salle's arrival, his brother's Catholic order granted La Salle a seigneury, or estate, at the western end of Montreal. He named it La Chine (later called Lachine), which is French for "China," and began to build a village and learn the local Indian language. But La Salle's true interests lay in exploration. When the Indians told him of a great river to the south called the Ohio, which flowed into the Mississippi, he was certain it was the passage he sought to the Far East. Having no idea of North America's inland geography, he was somehow convinced that the Ohio River, with its westward flow, would lead to the Pacific.

La Salle prepared an expedition to locate the western passage to China along this route. To finance the venture, he sold his holdings at La Chine, and with a birchbark brigade of five canoes and twelve men he headed for the Ohio. In 1671, he claimed to have reached the river and followed it as far as present-day Louisville, Kentucky.

When La Salle returned to Quebec, Frontenac appointed him commander of Fort Frontenac, the fur-trading station on Lake Erie that was still under construction. After supervising a complete reconstruction of the fort and winning even greater favor with the governor, he and his friend Louis Hennepin, a Catholic friar, journeyed farther and farther south. Over the next few years they established posts on Lake Michigan and along the Illinois and Mississippi rivers, where they encouraged trade with the Indians in the area.

La Salle's far-flung fur-trade outposts became ideal hiding places for the unlicensed woods runners, who were masters at evading New France's taxes and regulations. Government officials and merchants, who opposed Frontenac's and La Salle's empire building, considered these fur traders to be uncivilized, hard-drinking hooligans. In frustration, they let their concerns be known to the French king.

Within months, Frontenac was recalled to France. The governor who replaced him favored controlling the fur trade from Montreal and Quebec, as did the merchants there who would profit from having all the trade funneled through their towns. Resistance to La Salle also came from the missionaries, who disliked the harmful influence of the woods runners at the distant posts where the priests were trying to save Indian souls.

The government went so far as to accuse La Salle of carrying on illegal trade with the western Indians and even trading with the English of New York. Amid this fierce opposition, La Salle lost his trading monopoly, or charter, that the king had granted him. With Frontenac called back to France and Indian wars raging in much of the trading territories, La Salle's prospects looked bleak. So he once again turned to his dream of finding a western route to China.

In 1682, accompanied by Indian guides and Father Hennepin, he headed a birchbark brigade that paddled across Lake Michigan, up the Chicago River to the Illinois River, and on into the Mississippi. They traveled down the river all the way to the Gulf of Mexico, claiming the entire watershed for France and naming it Louisiana after King Louis XIV. Although China was nowhere in sight, La Salle guessed that if he could construct a trading post at the mouth of the Mississippi, he could bypass all the trading restrictions and licenses of New France that had recently plagued him. He would deal directly with European merchants. To him, this idea seemed almost as good as finding a passage to China.

This 1870s lithograph by Jean-Adolphe Bocquin illustrates René-Robert Cavelier, Sieur de La Salle, at the mouth of the Mississippi River claiming Louisiana for France in 1682.

Filled with self-importance and dressed in a gold-laced red cloak, La Salle ordered a cross planted and a plate buried under it bearing the name of Louis XIV. The official report of the ceremony records the words proclaimed by the explorer who had just extended New France to the edge of the Spanish Empire:

"I, René-Robert Cavelier de La Salle, by virtue of His Majesty's commission … have taken and do now take, in the name of His Majesty and of his successors to the crown, possession of the country of Louisiana, the seas, harbours, ports, bays, adjacent straits, and all the nations, peoples, provinces, cities, towns, villages, mines, minerals, fisheries, streams and rivers, within the extent of the said Louisiana."

At the same time that La Salle was extending the boundaries and the possibility of the fur trade south of the Great Lakes and claiming the entire Mississippi River basin for France, another woods runner had begun trading farther north and west into the country of the Dakota, or Sioux, Indians. His name was Daniel Greysolon Duluth, a Frenchman of noble birth who arrived in Canada a few years after La Salle.

Like La Salle and so many before him, Duluth anticipated finding an overland route to the Pacific. He learned from the Dakota Indians that a twenty-day trip through a chain of lakes and rivers across the continent could lead to a salt ocean.

Although he never made the trip to what historians now theorize was the Great Salt Lake in Utah, he recorded the information in his journal. That helped keep alive the dream of finding the Northwest Passage for another fifty years.

In the meantime, Duluth explored and traded with the Dakota and Ojibwa Indians throughout the upper Midwest, including the headwaters of the Mississippi

In 1905, artist Douglas Volk painted this interpretation of Father Louis Hennepin naming the Falls of St. Anthony, located at present-day Minneapolis, Minnesota. The painting hangs in the Minnesota State Capitol in St. Paul.

in northern Minnesota. His trading empire stretched from his main post at the mouth of the Kaministiquia River on the north shore of Lake Superior to Lake Winnipeg and south to the Falls of St. Anthony at present-day Minneapolis. From his post on Lake Nipigon, he attracted many Indians from the north and seriously interfered with the English trade on Hudson Bay.

La Salle was resentful of Duluth's success in the north. When he returned to Canada from the Gulf of Mexico, he decided to go back to France and seek the

This is an eighteenth-century artist's rendering of La Salle's ships landing at Matagorda Bay, Texas, in 1684.

king's help to open up the fur trade on the Mississippi River. The great river highway could transport furs to France, he explained to the king. With its claim on the Gulf of Mexico, Spain might decide to take the Mississippi River valley and gain the fur trade of the Great Lakes, he warned. And then there were the English to worry about.

"Should foreigners anticipate us," La Salle told the king, "they will complete the ruin of New France, which they already hem in by their establishments in Virginia, Pennsylvania, New England, and Hudson's Bay." He predicted that the English would next found colonies on the upper Mississippi, which would gain them the fur trade of New France. He urged the French government to arm the Mississippi valley Indians so they would be drawn into a war against the Iroquois to the east.

All the arguments seemed to make sense, but the most compelling one involved using Louisiana as a base to take over the Spanish silver mines to the south and west. All La Salle needed to do to convince the king to fund another expedition was to alter the maps a bit so that the Mississippi River appeared closer to New Spain (Mexico). Who would know? And with a French settlement closer to the Spanish riches, the plan seemed feasible.

In 1684, after two years of preparation, La Salle sailed from France with four ships and three hundred crewmen and colonists intent on strengthening France's claim to Louisiana. Plagued by pirates, disease, a shortage of drinking water, and faulty navigation, the expedition seemed doomed from the start. One ship was lost to pirates in the West Indies; a second sank off the coast of Texas with much of the expedition's food, tools, and weapons; and a third returned to France with a mutinous, disgruntled crew.

La Salle was known to be bad-tempered and a harsh, arrogant leader who had a tendency to bend the truth. So when he missed the mouth of the Mississippi by nearly five hundred miles and ended up in Matagorda Bay near present-day Corpus Christi, Texas, there were rumblings of mutiny among the remaining crew.

The would-be colonists struggled ashore to the mosquito- and snake-infested coast and built a small post named Fort St. Louis. Disease, alligators, and conflicts with the local Karankawa Indians soon took the lives of most of them. The survivors were stranded when a squall blew their last remaining ship, the *Belle*, across Matagorda Bay, where it grounded on a muddy flat and slowly sank. La Salle set out on foot three different times to continue his search for the mouth of the Mississippi. But in his angry and single-minded efforts, he managed to alienate even those few men who still remained faithful to him. He was shot and killed by one of them the following spring, an event that led the Karankawa to sack Fort St. Louis and kill most of the remaining French settlers.

Of the three hundred people who began the expedition, only six, including La Salle's brother, Jean Cavelier, eventually made it back to France through Canada. La Salle's body was never found.

Back in New France, Frontenac had been replaced by two ineffective leaders, one after another, who only managed to make the Iroquois more defiant and the English more determined to extend their fur trading farther west. Even the woods runners, who hated the Iroquois, helped those Indians turn piles of beaver skins over to the English. With the price for beaver so much higher at Albany, the French governor himself was accused of trading with the English.

The French king sent Frontenac back to New France in 1689. Buoyed by this renewed support, he was determined to defeat the Iroquois and invade New England and New York. The war that followed was named King William's War. An

Cofferdams are routinely built for bridge construction but are seldom used to excavate sunken ships. As the oldest French shipwreck discovered in the Western Hemisphere, La Salle's ship held huge historical significance and was excavated using a cofferdam.

Finding La Salle's Ship

In 1995, after years of searching, La Salle's ship the *Belle* was discovered in Matagorda Bay, Texas. Encased in gray, gooey mud that helped seal it from decay, the wreck lay in twelve feet of water. Realizing that it was one of the most important shipwrecks ever found in North America, the Texas Historical Commission funded the excavation of the three-hundred-year-old relic.

To unearth the ship and its artifacts, a steel structure called a cofferdam was built to encircle the site. Workers pumped tons of seawater out of the cofferdam until the wreckage was exposed on dry land. Then archaeologists began the year-long job of retrieving the artifacts.

Most of the ship's stores—wooden boxes jammed with trade goods, casks lined with muskets, miles of woven rope, cannons, dishes, and more—were found in remarkably good condition. Here, for the first time, was an intact seventeenth-century French colonizing kit containing everything needed to establish a trading post in the New World. Even the ship's hull and timbers were still preserved, waterlogged and fragile but looking very much like they did when La Salle last saw them. The timbers still bore the original numbers scrawled into each of them to aid the ship's builders in assembling the *Belle*. The one million artifacts represent a seventeenth-century time capsule.

extensive attack on the British colonies never took place, but for the next nine years constant skirmishes between Frontenac's troops and the Iroquois, along with raids on New England outposts, turned most of Iroquois country into a war zone.

In response, the British sent a fleet of thirty-four warships from Boston to capture the French colony. Under the command of Admiral William Phips, the ships sailed up the St.

This 1925 watercolor by Canadian artist C. W. Jefferys depicts Governor Frontenac (center right) receiving the messenger sent by Admiral Phips at Fort St. Louis, 1690.

Lawrence toward Quebec, where Frontenac had mustered all the soldiers he could find as well as most of the townspeople. When Phips sent Major Thomas Savage as an envoy to demand Quebec's surrender, Frontenac ordered the man blindfolded and brought to his headquarters.

As Savage was led through the streets, the citizens and soldiers raised a rowdy commotion pretending that the town was crowded with troops and bristling for a fight. The blindfolded soldier was jostled by the mob and confused by all the noise. It seemed to him Quebec had a huge military force that was ready for battle. When he was brought before Frontenac and his blindfold was removed, Savage was surprised to find the governor and his officers in their most elegant uniforms. This appeared to be a serious, organized enemy. When Savage read Admiral Phips's demand for surrender, Frontenac shot back: "My only reply to your general will be from the mouth of my cannons!"

Two days later, on October 18, 1690, fourteen hundred British troops landed at Beauport, east of the city, and lined up to attack the mighty and organized army of New France. The Battle of Quebec lasted less than three days. The English forces, muddled and intimidated by Frontenac's psychological tactic that made them think

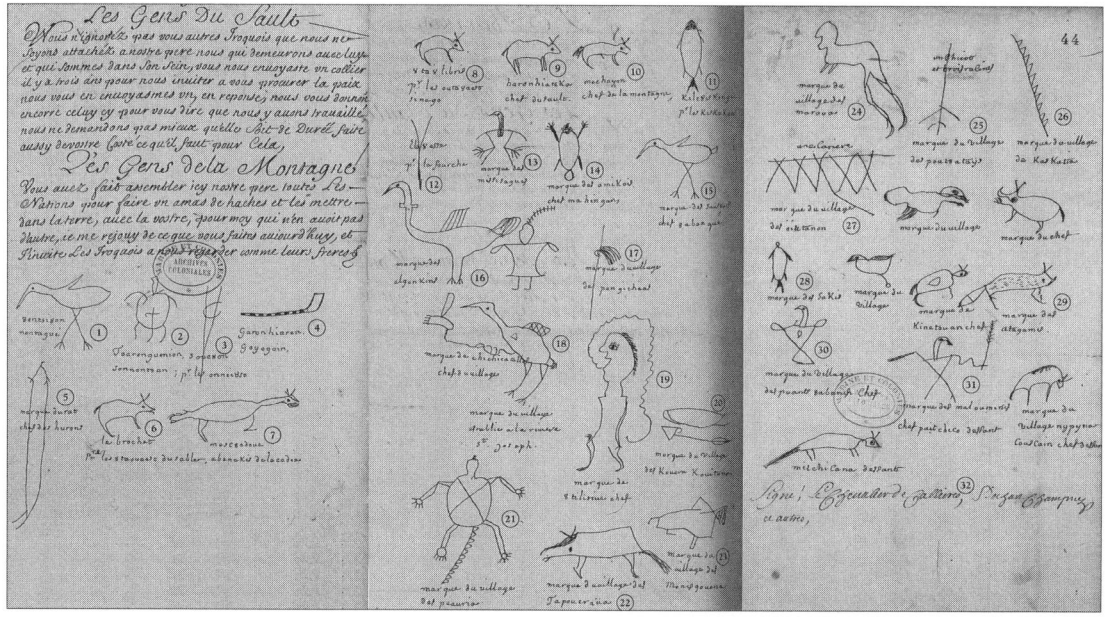

On August 4, 1701, the Great Peace treaty was signed between French colonists and thirty-nine different Indian tribes, ending for a time the decades of bloody conflict between the French and Iroquois. Each chief signed the document by drawing the totemic animal of his tribe.

they were outnumbered, were pounded by the French. In near panic, they retreated on October 22, abandoning five field guns on the shore as they sailed away.

In the next few years, Frontenac attempted to destroy the English fur trade to the south. With a series of complicated wars raging in Europe between France and England, France and Holland, and France and nearly every other European power that opposed the country's imperialism, French export trade in furs was seriously damaged. Bales upon bales of beaver pelts for which there was no market piled up in French storehouses and rotted. English furs from Hudson's Bay Company became more marketable, and there was a better demand for New York pelts. To restore New France's fur trade, Frontenac planned to invade the British colonies and crush the Iroquois at the same time.

The series of conflicts were called the Beaver Wars. Over the next few years, the French colonial soldiers learned how to fight in the woods and finally made headway at pushing back the Iroquois. The Iroquois attempted to defend themselves against the French and at the same time attack neighboring tribes in order to seize more of the trade. Many Indian nations living in present-day Ohio, Indiana, Michigan, and Ontario fled for refuge to remote parts of the west. The Sauk, Fox, Potawatomi, Kickapoo, Ottawa, Miami, and Huron were pushed out of their lands. Within a generation, the Ohio Valley was vacant.

When Frontenac died in 1698, the Iroquois, who saw themselves caught in the middle of a conflict between the French and the English, sued for peace. The Great Peace was signed in Montreal in 1701 by thirty-nine Indian chiefs, which included leaders from the Five Nations of the Iroquois, the Algonquin, Ottawa, Ojibwa, Cree, Abenaki, Miami, Potawatomi, and Wyandot, and colonial French and English government officials. In the treaty, the Iroquois agreed to stop marauding and to allow Indians who had moved west to areas around Wisconsin to return east.

It was a short-lived peace. France, Great Britain, and Spain considered all of North America up for grabs. With so much territory at stake and so much potential wealth and power to be gained, the three rivals continued to battle over territory for the next fifty years. Great Britain fought Spain in Florida and France in Nova Scotia during Queen Anne's War from 1702 to 1713. In King George's War, from 1744 to 1748, France joined with Spain against Great Britain. The details of the conflicts aren't as important as how they caused a growing frustration and hatred between New France and the English colonists.

In the years that followed, the English colonies south of New France began to build their economies on other businesses in addition to the fur trade. Although the trade continued, shipbuilding and other industries offered better investment opportunities for some. More land in the western frontier beyond the Allegheny Mountains was cleared for farming, and English settlements crept constantly westward into land that belonged to the Iroquois but was claimed by both France and Great Britain. Fur traders from New France and the English colonies competed bitterly over trading rights in the lands between the Alleghenies and the Mississippi River. This competition and other international conflicts between the two nations led to the French and Indian War in 1754.

CHAPTER 5

"A Stranger to the Commerce"

By 1753, French traders had moved into the western edge of Virginia as French soldiers continued to build a chain of military posts from Canada to the Ohio River. In the process they took possession of the Ohio country and pushed out English troops and fur traders.

The Iroquois tribes that inhabited the region had to begin trading with the French instead of the English. But trading with the French seemed like a bad deal. The Iroquois had to offer more furs to buy goods, and the goods were poorer in quality than those of the British.

A group of English colonists who had formed the Ohio Land Company in 1747 were granted a large tract of land north of the Ohio River. They were furious that the French were building forts in the same region. Virginia's royal lieutenant governor, Robert Dinwiddie, decided something had to be done. He wrote a letter to the commander of the French forces on the Ohio demanding them to leave, and he assigned a twenty-one-year-old volunteer soldier named George Washington to deliver it.

In October 1753, Washington, along with Christopher Gist, a well-known Virginia frontiersman; Jacob Van Braam, a Dutchman who could speak French; two servants; and two Indian traders left Williamsburg, Virginia, for the Ohio country. On his trip west, Washington met with various Indian tribes and finally reached Fort Le Boeuf near Lake Erie.

He was invited to dine privately with the French commander, Legardeur de Saint-Pierre, to whom he presented Lieutenant Governor Dinwiddie's letter. Washington wrote in his journal, "They told me, That it was their absolute Design to take Possession of the Ohio, and by G—— they would do it. ... They pretend to have an undoubted Right to the River, from a Discovery made by one LaSalle 60 Years ago. ..."

The French refused to back down, and Washington's party began their return

The Ohio Land Company

In 1747, a group of well-to-do Virginia planters formed the Ohio Land Company to invest in lands west of the Appalachian Mountains. They planned to purchase a large tract, subdivide it, and sell parcels to settlers for profit. They were also interested in participating in the area's lucrative fur trade, which was mostly controlled by the French.

A charter was granted to the company in 1749 that secured rights to two hundred thousand acres near the forks of the Ohio River. The company promised to settle one hundred families in the territory and build a fort to protect them and Great Britain's claim to the region.

In 1750, Christopher Gist was sent by the Ohio Land Company to explore and survey the land in preparation for settlement. But almost immediately the French began building forts in the area, determined to stop Britain from gaining a foothold on land that France had already claimed.

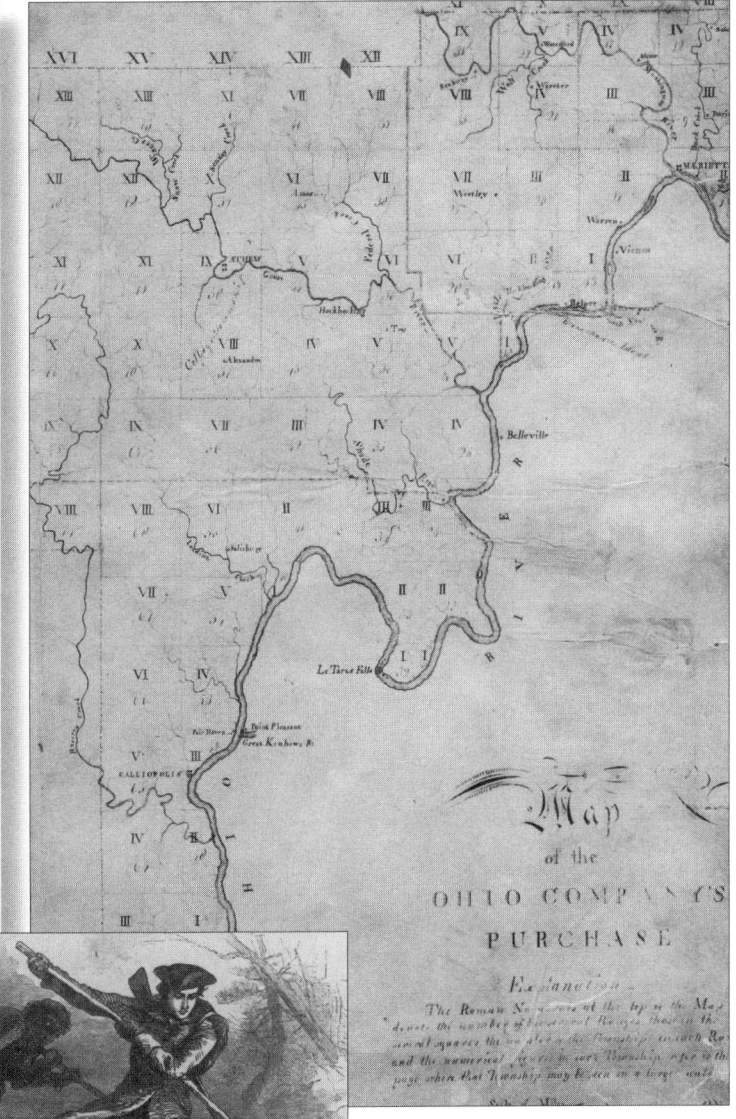

ABOVE In 1749, the Ohio Land Company's territory encompassed two hundred thousand acres on the condition that the company would, within seven years, settle one hundred families in the area and erect a fort to protect both them and Great Britain's claim on the land.

LEFT This woodcut by New York artist Daniel P. Huntington shows a young George Washington (right) and Christopher Gist crossing the icy Allegheny River in 1753.

journey to Virginia in the dead of winter. The bitter cold, deep snow, ice, and freezing rain made the trek nearly unbearable. Washington wrote: "Our horses were now so weak and feeble, and the Baggage heavy. ... therefore myself and others gave up our Horses for Packs. ..." Washington dressed himself in Indian clothing so he would be less noticeable, and then he and Christopher Gist returned to Virginia on foot. While traveling through the woods, they ran into an Indian ambush. One of them—"not 15 Steps away," wrote Washington—fired at the pair but missed. Washington recorded that the weather was so severe that Gist froze all his fingers and some of his toes.

When they finally arrived back in Williamsburg on January 16, 1754, Washington spent the entire next day writing an account of his trip made from the notes he had scribbled while traveling. The journal was presented to the Virginia Assembly the following morning, and the group immediately raised a regiment of three hundred men to defend the frontier and maintain Great Britain's rights over the Ohio valley. Two months later the *Maryland Gazette* published Washington's account in two installments, and copies of the report traveled all the way to London.

The English colonists were not about to let the French take over the Ohio Valley. In April 1754, Washington once again marched west, this time with 150 troops and orders to build a wider road over the Allegheny Mountains so that wagons and artillery could be rolled into the disputed area.

George Washington's detailed account of his trip to the Ohio country in the fall of 1753 appeared in two installments of the Maryland Gazette *in the spring of 1754.*

He and his troops were told to take the "Lands on the Ohio; & the Waters thereof." His destination was the strategic location at the forks of the Ohio River—the peninsula created by the confluence of the Allegheny, the Monongahela, and the Ohio rivers—the site of present-day Pittsburgh. Washington didn't know that the French had beaten him to the spot, constructing Fort Duquesne that same month.

On May 23, 1754, the French at Fort Duquesne sent out a scouting party of thirty-five troops headed by Joseph Coulon de Jumonville. Iroquois scouts discovered them traveling southwest toward the road-building troops from Virginia and reported the fact to Half-King, a local Indian leader allied with Washington and the English. Half-King went to Washington and pleaded with him to attack the French. The English encampment at Great Meadows, a flat, marshy clearing in the woods, was only a short night's march from the scouting party.

On the foggy, rain-soaked morning of May 28, forty of Washington's soldiers, assisted by Half-King and a band of Iroquois warriors, surrounded the French encampment. Within fifteen minutes, twenty-one Frenchmen were captured, twelve were killed, and Jumonville lay wounded. As Washington attempted to question the officer, Half-King walked up and, without warning, struck Jumonville in the head with a tomahawk, killing him.

George Washington's May 28, 1754, attack on Joseph Coulon de Jumonville's troops is depicted in Edward Sylvester Ellis's history book The Indian Wars of the United States, *published in 1896.*

When word of the incident reached Fort Duquesne, Jumonville's half brother, Captain Louis Coulon de Villiers, vowed revenge. He attacked Washington's troops at the hastily built Great Meadows garrison named Fort Necessity and forced the English to surrender on July 3, 1754. Washington was heavily criticized in Britain for the incident. British writer and statesman Horace Walpole referred to the controversy surrounding Jumonville's death as the "Jumonville Affair" and described it as "a volley fired by a young Virginian in the backwoods of America [that] set the world on fire."

They were the first shots of the French and Indian War. The fur trade in all of North America came to a halt as small skirmishes and larger battles broke out everywhere. The war widened from North America to Europe, where it was called the Seven Years' War. After nearly seven years, dozens of battles, and thousands of lives lost, the war came to the doorsteps of Montreal, the city on the St. Lawrence River founded by Samuel de Champlain.

That summer of 1760, Alexander Henry, a twenty-two-year-old from New Jersey, followed British general Jeffrey Amherst's army up the St. Lawrence toward the French colonial capital of Montreal. His flat-bottomed supply boat held food, ammunition, and other provisions for the British army as it made its way toward its final victory over New France.

This 1785 oil painting of Alexander Henry by an unknown artist shows Henry the businessman years after his first adventures into fur country.

Amherst's huge army of nearly seventeen thousand men attacked Montreal from three directions, eliminating any chance for the French to escape. With little more than two thousand men defending the capital, the French burned their flag rather than surrender it to Amherst. It was the last battle of the French and Indian War, and with Montreal's surrender, a whole new world opened up to young Alexander Henry.

After the battle, Henry rushed to Albany, New York, the center of the English fur trade. He obtained a trading permit from the British colonial government and headed north again to make his fortune in furs. "Proposing to avail myself of the new market, which was thus thrown open to British adventure …," he wrote, "I procured a quantity of goods."

Even though a peace treaty between the French and the English wouldn't be signed for another three years, Henry returned to Montreal, the center of the French fur trade. It was here that the birchbark brigades of traders and canoes assembled, and within a few days he was paddling west toward the Great Lakes. Unfortunately, the young trader was generally ignorant of everything related to the trade. "I was altogether a stranger to the commerce in which I was engaging," he admitted.

Luckily, Henry hired an experienced French fur trader by the name of Campion to train him. But even though Montreal was now in the hands of Amherst's soldiers, with no peace treaty signed, Great Britain and France were still at war. France's Indian allies remained hostile to any Englishman who ventured into the area. On his way west, Indians repeatedly warned the new fur trader that the Ojibwa tribesmen would consider him an enemy and probably kill him. But by the time Henry seriously considered heeding their warning, his supplies were so low that he couldn't go back to where he had come from.

So he took off his European-style clothing, pulled on deerskin leggings, a shirt, and a sash, and disguised himself as a voyageur—a canoe-paddling laborer. He convinced his friend Campion to act as the trader. "I had the satisfaction to find that my disguise enabled me to pass several canoes without attracting the smallest notice," he wrote. However, when his brigade arrived at Fort Michilimackinac, the main trading center on the route west, he must have thought his disguise wasn't quite good enough to risk walking about the post. He immediately hid out in a cabin, hoping to avoid detection.

Fort Michilimackinac had been built by the French on the south shore of the Straits of Mackinac—the narrows between Lake Huron and Lake Michigan—in 1715. Since then, it had served as a supply post for French traders operating in the western Great Lakes region and as a primary stopping-off point between Montreal

Reconstruction of this fort, originally built by the French from 1714 to 1715 to control the fur trade of the upper Great Lakes, began in 1960. Work on the fort has continued every summer since then, making Fort Michilimackinac the longest-running archaeological dig in North America.

and the western country. With the war over, the Ojibwa Indians of the area found the British policies harsh compared with those of the French, and they resented the British takeover.

When newcomer Alexander Henry arrived at the fort, the Ojibwa weren't fooled by his disguise and soon sought him out. "At two o'clock in the afternoon," Henry wrote, "[they] came to my house, about sixty in number, and headed by Minavavana, their chief. They walked in single file, each with his tomahawk in one hand, and scalping-knife in the other." Henry was petrified. The chief, a towering man of fifty years, stared steadfastly at the masquerading voyageur.

"Englishman," he said, "you know that the French king is our father. He promised to be such; and we, in return, promised to be his children. ... Englishman, although you have conquered the French, you have not yet conquered us! We are not your slaves. These lakes, these woods and mountains, were left to us by our ancestors. They are our inheritance; and we will part with them to none. ... Englishman, your king has never sent us any presents, nor entered into any treaty with us, wherefore he and we are still at war."

Rigid with fear and with his heart in his throat, Henry cast about for a response. Through an interpreter he explained to the chief "that it was the good character, which I had heard of the Indians, that had alone emboldened me to come among them." He told Minavavana that he came to "furnish them with necessaries, and that their good treatment of me would be an encouragement to others [traders]."

Henry was allowed to go free and Minavavana announced that he would treat Henry like a brother. The chief was impressed with the trader's openness and the fact that he carried no weapons.

Less than two years later, Henry was caught once again at Michilimackinac when Ottawa chief Pontiac organized an uprising against the British posts in the northwest. Infuriated by the disrespectful, patronizing attitude of the English, and secretly encouraged by Frenchmen who were still scattered among them, Pontiac and his followers formed a conspiracy to massacre all the English garrisons and settlers along the frontiers of Virginia, Pennsylvania, and the Great Lakes.

Pontiac visited many of the tribes and convinced them by using his extraordinary persuasiveness. He was an imposing warrior—tall, strong, and heavily tattooed in the custom of the Ottawa. He fashioned his straight black hair in a narrow, spiky comb like a kingfisher and wore silver bracelets on his arms and a collar of white plumes around his neck. He was known for his courage and effective speaking skills, and he commanded respect far beyond his own people.

Although Ottawa warrior chief Pontiac's conspiracy failed to push the English out of his tribe's territory, eight out of twelve central fur posts attacked by his followers in 1763 were destroyed. Terrified survivors of the massacre vacated the area.

He sent messengers to the tribes he couldn't visit himself, each representative bearing a wampum belt and a red-stained hatchet. Almost every tribe of the great Algonquin family and one tribe of the Five Nations, the Seneca, joined the conspiracy. So skillfully was the plot managed that the attack was made almost simultaneously in all regions, and every English post, except Detroit, Fort Pitt, and Niagara, fell into the hands of the Indians.

It was a sunny, late spring morning in 1763 when a group of Indians began a friendly game of lacrosse just outside the British post where Alexander Henry was staying. Several Indian women gathered to watch the game, heavy woolen blankets wrapped around them against the chilly air. Before the British knew what hit them, the players grabbed guns from under the women's blankets and stormed the fort. Henry was taken prisoner but once again was saved by another adopted Ojibwa brother, Chief Wawatam. After the attack, he lived with Wawatam's people for over a year, learning the Ojibwa language and more skills necessary for the fur trade.

Pontiac had managed to form a confederation of tribes that were united in their attempts to drive out the British. The Indians captured eight forts in present-day Michigan, Indiana, and Ohio. The brutal war lasted less than two years, but in the process over 450 British soldiers were killed along with many Indians, settlers, and traders. Because of the violence, most of the settlers who lived west of the Appalachian Mountains scurried back to the colonies. The war finally ended in 1765 when two thousand Indians met British officials at Fort Niagara and signed a peace treaty. The fur trade once again flourished in areas that had been vacated by the settlers.

In this drawing made in 1825 of Nicholas Vincent Isawanhonhi, principal chief of the Huron Indians, the chief holds up a wampum belt, a key communication tool of many Indian tribes.

This massive canoe, drawn in 1876 to illustrate a book on the history of the fur trade, is similar to the canoes Alexander Henry's men paddled in 1775.

Wampum

Wampum were small tubular shell beads strung together on a string and woven into belts. They were used by Indians of many tribes to note significant events in their history. Woven belts recorded ideas, contracts, pledges, treaties, or compacts between tribes. The exchange of wampum became an important part of diplomatic protocol whenever Indians and European colonists concluded a treaty or assembled for other councils.

The Iroquois attached great importance to the mystical power of the beads. Strings of wampum were used to sanction council proceedings, to vouch for the integrity of a speaker, to give responsibility to an office, or to honor a treaty. Messages of particular importance were also made into strings and sent by runners among the Iroquois. Various designs of beads indicated different ideas according to an accepted system that could be read by anyone acquainted with wampum language, no matter what his spoken language was. Some of the original wampum belts still exist and are now held by the Iroquois chiefs at Onondaga, New York.

At about the same time, Alexander Henry and his new partner, Jean Baptiste Cadotte, the son of a Canadian woods runner, were granted exclusive rights by the British colonial authorities to trade on Lake Superior. Over the next ten years, Henry's knowledge of the Ojibwa language and customs allowed him to extend his trade routes north into Canada. By 1775, he arrived at the trading post of Grand Portage on the western shore of Lake Superior with a brigade of sixteen canoes and fifty-two men, ready to capture an even greater part of the fur trade.

Grand Portage, or the "great carrying place," had been known to the Indians of the region for thousands of years. The fur

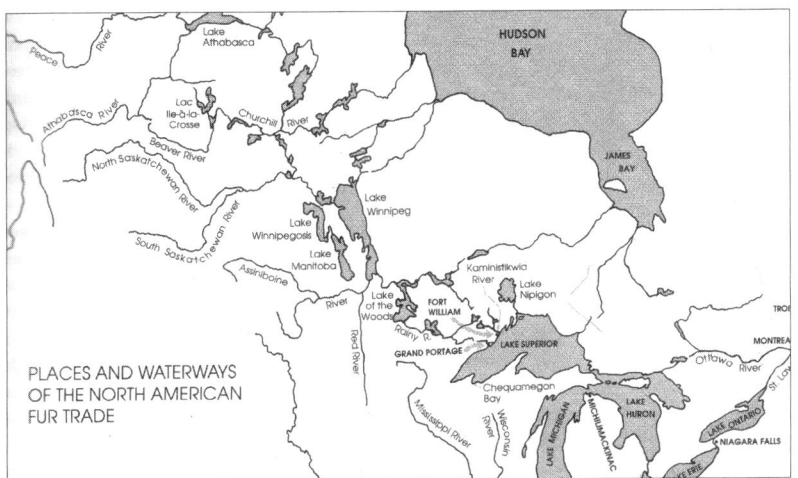

Although the North American fur trade extended across the entire continent, this map shows the focus of the trade in its heyday during the eighteenth century.

post sat next to a long, well-beaten path that led to the beginning of a network of lakes and streams that branch out across most of the continent. Located near the geographical heart of North America, Grand Portage, by 1775, was the epicenter of North American trade. From here, a person with a birchbark canoe and a lot of energy could reach the Atlantic, the Pacific, the Gulf of Mexico, Hudson Bay, or the Arctic Ocean without a single portage much longer than the eight-and-a-half-mile-long Grand Portage itself. And from here, trade goods from around the world were distributed to the far-flung outposts dotting every navigable river to the south, west, and north of Grand Portage.

So Who Were the Algonquin?

The Algonquin Indians refer to dozens of tribes who spoke languages that were closely related to one another. The Algonquin language group was one of the largest in native America. The Sauk, Shawnee, Potawatomi, Miami, Delaware, Ottawa, and Ojibwa tribes along with many others spoke related languages and lived across North America from the Atlantic Ocean to the Rocky Mountains and from northern Canada to the Carolinas. Most of the Algonquin tribes allied themselves with the French until France lost all its North American colonies after the French and Indian War.

CHAPTER 6

"I Now Mixed Up Some Vermilion in Melted Grease"

This sketch of Grand Portage, the western supply depot for the North West Company from 1778–1802, shows the post's sixteen buildings flanked by the campsites of the voyageurs and traders.

In the summer of 1775, Henry met another American fur trader at Grand Portage. His name was Peter Pond, a shoemaker's son from Milford, Connecticut. A tough, quarrelsome character who at the age of sixteen had left home to fight in the French and Indian War, Pond headed west at the war's end to trade for furs along the Mississippi River. He eventually made his way north to Grand Portage and beyond. Most considered him a loner and an eccentric, though "he thought himself a philosopher," one trader wrote, "and was odd in his manners."

Pond did have at least one odd inclination: killing people. He was accused of fighting a duel with a rival fur trader, which he won. And years later, he was charged with ordering his men to shoot another trader during a quarrel. He was never convicted in either case, but it was probably just as well that Pond had such a hankering for the far northwest. It helped keep him away from other people.

When Henry and Pond arrived at Grand Portage in 1775, they "found the traders in a state of extreme reciprocal hostility," Henry wrote. One historian described the fur post as a "pent-up hornets' nest of conflicting factions intrenched in rival forts." Rough rascals used to surviving in the toughest conditions lured each others' employees away, stole furs from one another, defaulted on debts, and sold liquor to the Indians. In short, the fur trade in Grand Portage was a bit of a free-for-all and not very conducive to a steady profit.

Henry and Pond along with several other traders decided to organize their business more effectively with the thought of edging out some of their competitors. When the traders met at Grand Portage in the summer of 1779, they pooled their goods and capital to help keep the pelts arriving from the interior and the trade goods arriving from London to Montreal. Five years later, they formalized the agreement, divided all their resources into sixteen shares, and named their new venture the North West Company. In the process, they divided up the known portions of the entire continent to create their trading regions.

Created around 1800, the North West Company coat of arms depicts a beaver at the top with the motto Perseverance. A canoe manned by voyageurs appears in the center of the emblem.

When it was first organized, the North West Company traded in the Great Lakes area of what is now the United States and Canada, and that trade region was twice as large as the trade region farther to the north. But the beaver southwest of Grand Portage couldn't compare in quality or quantity with northern beaver, and the successful American Revolution had opened the door to more and more settlers. The traders knew that when settlers moved in, the fur-bearing animals moved out. So the fur trade slowly shifted north into Canada.

The North West Company was based in Montreal, the center of the fur trade at the time. Its leaders initially included American fur traders Alexander Henry, Peter Pond, three English brothers named Frobisher, several other experienced traders,

This portrait of the head of the North West Company was painted in 1800 at the height of his power as the merchant of Montreal.

Simon McTavish

One of Peter Pond's financial partners in the North West Company was a young Highland Scot by the name of Simon McTavish, who had come to America penniless at the age of thirteen. By the time he was twenty-one in 1771, he was in business for himself, shipping rum from Albany, New York, to the important trading depot of Detroit. Described as a "charming young man who loved good wine, good oysters and pretty girls," McTavish had a passion for business. He moved to Montreal in 1775 and worked for several years to convince the competitive and disorganized traders that they could benefit from banding together. He proposed that if the traders went into business with him, they would become wealthy.

In the following decade, as the head of the North West Company, McTavish became the most powerful man in the fur trade. By the 1790s, more than a hundred huge canoes paddled inland from Montreal each spring. McTavish was that city's richest merchant.

and a merchant named Simon McTavish. These men weren't afraid to risk everything to get the pelts. Instead of waiting for the Indians to bring them furs, they brought the trade goods to the wilderness and bartered directly with the tribes, much like the woods runners a century before.

Unlike the Hudson's Bay Company that had been formed one hundred years earlier, the North West Company wasn't bound by rules established in Great Britain. The owners encouraged the traders to befriend the Indians and even marry into their families. Everyone understood that the success of their business completely depended on that relationship.

The North West Company had three levels of management. McTavish and other merchants in Montreal owned a controlling interest in the company and were at the top. They arranged for the importation of trade goods and marketed the furs abroad. At the second level, the wintering partners like Pond, Henry, and the Frobisher brothers were part owners in the business but lived year-round in the fur country away from Montreal. The wintering partners served as the company's representatives to the Indians. On the third level were the clerks who kept the books and hoped to someday have the opportunity to buy a share in the company. They sometimes managed smaller trading posts.

It was a tough, risky business. Each fall, the Montreal merchants like McTavish placed their orders for trade goods with an exporting house in London. The orders traveled by sailing ship across the Atlantic and arrived there several months later. By spring, the goods were packed, insured, and shipped back to Montreal. By the time they arrived in June, it was too late for them to be repacked into the birchbark canoes and transported west that season. The rivers and lakes beyond Grand Portage would have begun to freeze before the goods could be transported that far. So everything was stored in Montreal warehouses and then repacked in ninety-pound bales for shipment the following spring.

With two ocean crossings and a half-year delay while goods sat stacked in Montreal warehouses, money invested in the business took a full two years or more before turning a profit. And things didn't always go as planned. Orders for merchandise got lost, canoes were wrecked, ships sank, and storms and early freeze-ups stopped travel.

In one good year, the North West Company brought in 160,000 beaver pelts along with many thousands of other furs—nearly four times as much as their competitor, the Hudson's Bay Company. Shareholders like Henry, Pond, the Frobishers, and McTavish became wealthy.

But not everyone had joined the North West Company. For the next three years, traders from competing partnerships fought and undercut each other until the winter of 1786–87, when John Ross, a rival trader, was shot in a scuffle with Pond's men.

TOP Cloth and blankets were key items during the fur trade. Here a trader at Montreal displays his wares to his customers.

ABOVE View of the Harbour, Montreal, 1830 by Robert Auchmuty Sproule depicts the bustling port where trade goods from Europe arrived and furs from the interior were loaded on ships bound for the hat makers of Paris and London.

News of the death prompted the leaders of several trading companies to unite and end the murderous competition.

Along with managing rivalries, competition, and shifting supplies of furs, some explorers and traders still searched for a waterway that would take them through the continent to the Pacific Ocean. Peter Pond was obsessed with the idea of finding that passage since first wintering in northern Canada in the 1770s. When he opened up the Athabaska country in present-day northern Saskatchewan to the fur trade in 1779, he intercepted Indians on their way to trade with the Hudson's Bay Company at Fort Prince of Wales. Pleased to avoid traveling so far, the Indians gladly traded with Pond, and by spring he found himself with more pelts than his canoes could carry. He hid some and returned for them later.

In the next few years, Pond explored even farther north into Canada and continued to draw maps of his findings. By 1787, he was forty-seven years old and considered an old man in the fur trade. That winter a new, young wintering partner of the North West Company named Alexander Mackenzie joined Pond at Fort Chipewyan.

Mackenzie had immigrated with his father to New York from Scotland when he was a young boy. During the American Revolution, he was sent to school in Montreal, where he soon joined a fur trading company as a clerk. When that company united with the North West Company, Mackenzie went along as a partner and was stationed with Pond. All through that frostbitten winter, Pond redrew and explained his Canadian maps to the young trader. Although Pond was completely convinced that the Pacific lay within easy reach of their wintering post, his drawings proved to have some major flaws.

The following winter, Pond had to return to Montreal to face murder charges after a run-in with a fellow trader, and twenty-four-year-old Mackenzie was promoted to manage Fort Chipewyan, then the largest and most important

Scottish-born Alexander Mackenzie began working for a Montreal fur-trading company at the age of fifteen. When it merged with the North West Company in 1785, it gave him the opportunity to join Peter Pond at the far northern post of Fort Chipewyan, setting the stage for more explorations west.

department of the North West Company. One of his main objectives that winter was to interrupt the trade between the pelt-trading Indian tribes of the area and the Hudson's Bay Company at the fur depot named York Factory. While he managed the fur trade, he made plans for exploring the Northwest Passage.

Finally on June 3, 1789, he set out from Fort Chipewyan with five experienced voyageurs and two Indian women. The women would make and mend clothing, prepare food, and help with carrying supplies. Mackenzie had no idea where he was going. A frigid wind blustered from the northwest and then it began to snow. By June 9, after trudging across six swampy portages and losing one canoe, they reached Great Slave Lake and found it still frozen. The group camped there for nearly a month before they finally were able to paddle down a huge river toward what Mackenzie hoped was the Pacific.

On July 14, 1789, Mackenzie and his tattered brigade reached the Arctic Ocean. All through the first night, camped by the ocean, the sun never set and it was cold. Mackenzie was so heartbroken over ending up at the wrong ocean that he named the river that brought him there the River of Disappointment. It was later renamed the Mackenzie River.

This nineteenth-century image of a lake in the far north of Canada resembles Great Slave Lake, a lake that stays ice-covered for more than eight months of the year.

The next summer, he traveled to Grand Portage to attend the annual meeting of the North West Company and announce his discovery. When Peter Pond heard that the huge new river he had drawn on his maps didn't flow to the Pacific and his calculations had been all wrong, he was so disappointed that he quit the fur trade for good, sold his share in the company, and went to work for the U.S. government. Actually, no one in the North West Company was very impressed with Mackenzie's discovery.

Mackenzie was convinced that he needed more knowledge of surveying and astronomy if he were to become a successful explorer. He sailed to England for more mathematical training and better instruments. When he finally returned to Canada in 1793, he was better equipped and even more determined to find the Pacific Ocean through Canada.

But the fur trade had to come first. While making his exploration plans during the winter, he sent out scouts to visit Indian bands, feasted with the chiefs, handed out trade goods on credit, and took in pelts. In the early spring, he pressed and baled the pelts, ordered canoes built and repaired, and wrote careful reports of the trading season. Then he sent a brigade of six birchbark canoes downstream to Grand Portage while he stayed behind.

On May 9, 1793, Mackenzie along with a North West Company clerk named Alexander McKay; six voyageurs named Beauchamp, Beaulieux, Bisson, Courtois, Ducette, and Landry; and two Indians who would work as interpreters and hunters all squeezed into one canoe. The specially built craft was "so light, that two men could carry her on a good road three or four miles without resting," Mackenzie wrote. "In this slender vessel, we shipped provisions, goods for presents, arms, ammunition, and baggage, to the weight of three thousand pounds, and an equipage of ten people." The "provisions" included pemmican, a mixture of dried, pulverized buffalo meat; grease; and dried berries. It was an essential food that made the fur trade into northern Canada and the American West possible.

Every mile of the way was difficult, and many of the Indians they met refused to guide them. When a wrong river was followed, the group was forced to paddle back to the fork in the stream where the error had occurred and start in another direction.

By the end of June, the men were discouraged and worn out. But Mackenzie persuaded the group to paddle, pull, and portage on by sharing every hardship with his men and eating exactly the same meager rations. Sometimes they climbed trees to get a better view of where they were.

On July 4, they hid their canoe and some of their supplies and continued west on foot. Mackenzie's own load consisted of pemmican and other provisions weighing about seventy pounds, along with a gun, ammunition, and his telescope. The group traveled west on Indian paths most of the way and two weeks later came upon a small settlement of Bella Coola Indians that he named Friendly Village. Two days later, he came upon six curious Indian houses built on stilts nearly twenty-five feet high. "From these houses," Mackenzie wrote, "I could perceive the termination of the river, and its discharge into a narrow arm of the sea." He had reached the Pacific Ocean.

Mackenzie had managed to maintain friendly relations with all the Indians he had met on his journey. But as he approached the mouth of the Bella Coola River, the local Indians were anything but friendly. As a result, he and his men spent little time exploring. They found a canoe and paddled down Dean Channel. That night, July 21, they slept on a large rock in Dean Channel, and the next morning Mackenzie wrote in his journal: "I now mixed up some vermilion in melted grease and inscribed, in large characters, on the

Artist Eastman Johnson created this painting of Ojibwa women in 1857 when he was visiting relatives in the area around Grand Portage.

Pemmican

At the fur posts on the northern plains, buffalo hunting and pemmican making was a yearly routine. Indian women sliced fresh buffalo meat into thin strips and dried it over a slow fire. "Women employed all day Slicing and drying the meat" was a typical entry in a trader's journal. Then the meat was pounded into a thick, flaky mass, mixed with melted fat, and packed in buffalo-hide bags specially designed for the food.

The bags, weighing ninety pounds each, were sent to posts along the central waterways, where they were picked up by the voyageurs. They relied on four such sacks of pemmican to carry them about five hundred miles to the next post, where the voyageurs loaded their next ration. Pemmican didn't spoil and was so dense and nutritious that one pound was equal to four pounds of fresh meat.

South-East face of the rock on which we had slept last night this brief memorial—Alexander Mackenzie, From Canada, By Land, 22d July 1793."

A rock at Dean Channel in British Columbia, Canada, still bears a replica of the inscription painted by Alexander Mackenzie on his discovery of the Pacific Ocean in 1793.

The following morning, the group started for home, and in thirty-three days the ten men in one canoe "rounded a point, and came in view of the Fort. ... while the men were in such spirits, and made such an active use of their paddles, that we arrived before the two men whom we left here in the spring, could recover their senses to answer us. ... Here my voyages of discovery terminate," Mackenzie wrote in his final journal entry. "Their toils and their dangers, their solicitudes and sufferings, have not been exaggerated in my description. ... I received, however, the reward of my labours, for they were crowned with success."

A Northwest Passage had been discovered just over three hundred years after Columbus first sailed west to find it. Mackenzie returned to Grand Portage a hero. When the journals of his adventures were published in London a few years later, a copy was purchased by President Thomas Jefferson, an avid book collector and reader. It was Mackenzie's book on this overland voyage to the Pacific coupled with the recent U.S. acquisition of the Louisiana Purchase that prompted the president to launch the Lewis and Clark expedition.

A century and a half had passed since Samuel de Champlain first recognized how important the fur trade could be in North America. Now the business had grown so that it involved Indians and traders from all over the continent. Brigades of birchbark canoes paddled through the Great Lakes and the rivers and lakes that threaded across all of Canada and the newly formed United States.

CHAPTER 7

"A Fair Specimen of the Life"

With the North West Company organized and expanding, the fur trade boomed in the Great Lakes region. At the same time, the Hudson's Bay Company, located at outposts on the shores of Hudson Bay north of Lake Superior, began building trading posts inland to compete with the North West Company.

In the fall, each birchbark brigade of traders who had paddled from their summer rendezvous at Grand Portage built a North West Company post on a stream in the middle of Indian country. When the Indians arrived, they were given their choice of trade goods on credit. Then throughout the winter the Indians brought in beaver pelts and other furs plus meat and wild rice to pay for the trade goods. As soon as the ice cleared in the spring, the fur traders loaded their canoes with the bales of pressed and wrapped pelts collected through the winter. Then their brigade of birchbark canoes paddled once again toward Grand Portage where the entire company met for the rendezvous each July.

In the 1770s, the British were preoccupied with the discontented American colonists, who were fighting for their independence from Great Britain. But no one in fur country was paying much attention to the activities in Boston or Philadelphia. While it was being fought, the American Revolution in the colonies had little impact on the trade. Most of the furs and trade goods moved through Montreal and the rivers and lakes north of the British colonies. The fur trade region was so far removed from the battles to the south that when the Revolutionary War ended with the Treaty of Paris in 1783, it took nearly a year for the news to travel all the way to what is now Michigan.

The treaty gave the new United States control of most of the land east of the Mississippi River. The land west of the river had been ceded to Spain by France at the end of the French and Indian War. Before independence, four colonies (Virginia, New York, Connecticut, and Massachusetts) claimed portions of the Ohio region under their original charters. During the 1780s, they yielded the claims to the new federal government, and Congress defined the region as the Northwest Territory. All the land within it was to be sold in lots either to individuals or companies, and it was assumed that eventually the area would form as many as five states. Immediately the rush was on to subdivide, claim, and settle the new territories of the United States.

The opportunity for land had families from all over colonial America pushing through the mountains and spreading across the Ohio Valley. That the land was already inhabited by several Indian tribes seemed of little concern. Violent Kentucky frontiersmen began raiding Indian villages in the area. In response, chiefs of the Miami and Shawnee tribes, who were determined to keep the American intruders south of the Ohio River, began raiding the new American settlements. The fur trade was once again disrupted in the entire region.

Disputed treaties were ignored by Indians and settlers alike. By 1789, the fighting was so bad that to help keep the peace the U.S. government built Fort Washington on the north bank of the Ohio River at the site of present-day Cincinnati.

The only known portrait of John Tanner, this image appeared in the frontispiece of his account of life with the Ojibwa Indians, originally published in 1830.

That year, young John Tanner and his family settled near the mouth of the Big Miami River, not far from Fort Washington. One morning, less than two weeks after they had arrived, Tanner's father prepared to go to a nearby field to plant corn. He warned Tanner's stepmother and the children "that from the actions of the horses, he perceived there were Indians lurking about in the woods," Tanner recalled. "He said to me, 'John, you must not go out of the house to day.'"

But as the morning wore on, the nine-year-old was tired of being shut up in the tiny frontier cabin with his stepmother and brother and sisters. Through the window he could see his father in the field. Tanner walked about the cabin carrying his baby brother and pinched him repeatedly to make him cry.

Finally his exasperated stepmother took the baby, and Tanner watched for his chance to escape. In a few moments he was out the door and skulking along the side of the field toward a walnut tree near the woods. As he gathered some walnuts into his straw hat, he was "seized by both hands, and dragged off betwixt two [Indians]."

His Shawnee captors, a father and son named Manito-o-geezhik and Kish-kau-ko who lived at Lake Huron, had traveled all the way to Ohio to kidnap a replacement for Kish-kau-ko's brother, who had died. Replacing a dead child with a captive stolen from another tribe or settlement was a common practice at the time.

Several more Indians joined them as they hustled the youngster through the woods. Tanner fought to wrench his arms from the grasp of one of the Indians. "I had probably made some resistance, or done something to irritate this last, for he took me a little to one side, and drawing his tomahawk, motioned to me to look up," Tanner recalled. "I did as he directed, but Kish-kau-ko caught his hand as the tomahawk was descending, and prevented him from burying it in my brains." Thus began a two-year ordeal with the Shawnee family who finally decided Tanner was no good when he was caught sleeping while he was supposed to be working. They sold him to an Ojibwa woman named Net-no-kwa, whose son had recently died.

"My old Indian mother, ..." Tanner recalled, "protested vehemently against it. ... But these remonstrances had little influence, when Net-no-kwa arrived with considerable whiskey, and other presents. ... She was perfectly acquainted with the dispositions of those with whom she had to negotiate. Objections were made to the exchange until the contents of the keg had circulated for some time; then an additional keg, and a few more presents completed the bargain, and I was transferred to Net-no-kwa."

Tanner and Net-no-kwa and the rest of his Ojibwa family paddled and trekked hundreds if not thousands of miles in an area ranging from Lake Michigan all the way to Lake Winnipeg in present-day Manitoba, Canada, to trade and hunt. Net-no-kwa was regarded as the principal chief of her tribe and, according to Tanner, "was then advanced in years." She and her family called themselves the Anishinabe—"the people." Others called them the Ojibwa or Chippewa. By the 1780s, their tribe stretched across the woodlands of the Great Lakes region, and they were deeply involved in the fur trade.

Tanner spent thirty years with the Ojibwa. When he finally returned to search

This mid-nineteenth-century painting by American artist Seth Eastman illustrates an Indian woman dressing a deerskin.

for his original family, he ended up becoming an Indian interpreter and narrated his detailed survival story. Although told by an adopted Ojibwa, it became one of the only written accounts of Indian life during the fur-trade era.

New tools, weapons, cloth, and even liquor came into the lives of Net-no-kwa and her family through the trade. As they began to depend on these goods, they spent more time and energy trapping beavers and preparing furs. The furs were perishable. After a pelt was skinned from an animal, it could begin to mold or rot. So the pelts needed to be processed as soon as the animals were killed.

The first step in processing the beaver fur was done by Indian women, who washed each pelt to remove blood and dirt. Next, they scraped any remaining flesh and fat from the inside of the skin with a special tool. The last step of drying and stretching the nearly circular beaver skin involved lacing the edge of it onto a willow hoop. Once they dried, the pelts were stiff and hard as a board. Then they were removed from the hoop and traded.

By the time Tanner joined the family, Net-no-kwa was fully in charge and "had the direction in all affairs of any moment." When she traveled to the trading post, "she always carried a flag in her canoe," Tanner was told. "Whenever she came to Mackinac [Fort Michilimackinac], she was saluted by a gun from the fort."

The lives of small bands of Ojibwa like Net-no-kwa's family centered on the seasons of the year. Young men in the tribe were expected to learn how to hunt so they could provide food not only for their families but also for the wintering traders. After trading at Fort Michilimackinac the first year Tanner was with Net-no-kwa, she and her family headed to the woods to hunt, trap, and fish.

A few days later she announced, "It is time for our son to begin to learn to be a hunter." Starvation lurked at the edge of every frigid winter in fur-trading country, and survival depended on a variety of hunting skills. Tanner's Ojibwa father loaded a pistol and gave it to him with the promise that if he successfully shot a pigeon, he would immediately earn a larger gun and become a hunter.

Tanner recalled that nothing in his life had made him more anxious for success than that first hunt. With pistol in hand he headed away from the camp. When some pigeons landed on a bush close to him, he cocked his pistol, laid his

About 1860, Cornelius Krieghoff painted this image of an Indian hunter. Krieghoff was born in Amsterdam but spent most of his adult life in Canada and the United States. For several years he lived on an Indian reservation, where he sketched numerous images of Indian life that he later painted.

nose right up next to the gun barrel, and sighted in the bird. When he pulled the trigger, the gun's discharge bruised and bloodied his face, sent the pistol spinning off behind him, and killed the bird. "I ran home, carrying my pigeon in triumph. My face was speedily bound up; my pistol exchanged for a fowling-piece. ... Henceforth I began to be treated with more consideration, and was allowed to hunt often that I might become expert," he recalled.

In the spring, they moved to the maple forests to collect sap from the trees and boil it down into sugar. During the warm days and cold nights early in the season, the maple sap dripped out of sharp wooden spouts hammered into the trees by the family. Birchbark buckets were used to gather the sap, and it was boiled down by dropping hot rocks into birchbark containers. Maple sugar was the main seasoning for most food and was traded at the fur posts for supplies. Birchbark for canoes,

TOP *Ojibwa wigwams, similar to this one made of birchbark, could be dismantled and moved from one camp to the next.*

ABOVE *Seth Eastman painted this image of Ojibwa women gathering wild rice on a northern lake. Long poles were used to bend the stems of the rice over the canoe while the harvesters beat the grain onto the floor of the vessel.*

shelters, and containers was also cut and peeled from the trees in the spring.

In the summer, large groups of extended families—grandparents, parents, children, brothers, sisters, and cousins—camped together in the same area year after year. Men like Tanner spent their time fishing, hunting, and building new canoes. The women dried extra meat and fish, prepared animal skins for making clothing as well as for trading, and harvested berries and nuts from the woods.

Fall was ricing season. Wild rice grew on the edges of the shallow lakes that stretched across the Ojibwa lands and was one of their most important foods. Each family had its own special area for harvesting rice. During six weeks in late August and September, the families worked together to gather and store as much rice as possible. A successful harvest helped ensure the family's survival and that of the fur traders.

Tanner recalled the suffering the Ojibwa endured through tough winters. After tracking a bear for nearly three days, he became so hungry and cold that he couldn't even start a fire. "I was endeavouring to reconcile myself to the immediate approach of death which I thought inevitable, when these people unexpectedly found me, and helped me to return to camp. This is but a fair specimen of the life … during the winter. … It is only with the utmost exertion and activity that life can be sustained, and it not unfrequently happens that the strongest men, and the best hunters, perish of absolute hunger."

From the age of fifteen until his death thirteen years later, Swiss-born artist Peter Rindisbacher created more than 124 sketches and watercolors of Indians and animals in central Canada and the midwestern United States. This painting shows hunters near Winnipeg, Canada, spearing beaver.

Beavers

The beaver is North America's largest rodent (thirty to sixty pounds). It is most active at night and does not hibernate. It was hunted to near extinction during the fur-trade era but now is quite common again in many parts of the continent. Beavers use deep water as a defense against predators. They construct dams on small streams to create the deep water they need. Their dams are located and constructed with great engineering skill as are their lodges, which they normally access from underwater.

During the fur-trade period, many beavers were harvested in the winter, when the animal had the thickest fur. Hunters cut holes in the ice near a beaver lodge and lowered nets through the holes. Then one man broke apart the lodge with an ax. As the animals tried to escape, they were caught in the nets and killed.

In the summer, hunters often shot the beavers with guns or arrows. The beavers' land paths were baited with the animal's favorite food, fresh aspen twigs, and then traps or snares were set. Metal traps weren't used until the later years of the fur trade.

CHAPTER 8

"Slapped on the Face by a Grisly Bear"

This damaged photo taken in 1875 of a fur trapper on the north shore of Lake Superior shows him in winter clothing and snowshoes.

By the time John Tanner and his Ojibwa family were involved in the fur trade in the 1790s, there were several thousand voyageurs working for the North West Company. Joseph LaRose, Simon Chaurette, Pierre Biron—we know their names because they had to sign contracts before joining a canoe brigade at Montreal.

Most were illiterate farm boys from the small towns surrounding Montreal. Captivated by the opportunity for adventure and hoping to avoid the drudgery of life on the farm, boys as young as fifteen paddled with the older, more experienced men. With his swaggering strut, long hair, loud mouth, and brightly colored shirt and sash, an experienced voyageur was easy to spot. He often had a short pipe clamped in the corner of his mouth, and he greeted his comrades in French mixed with a few Ojibwa words and English expressions.

A voyageur's job was to paddle a canoe and carry cargo over portages—the patches of land between lakes, or paths along impassable portions of rivers. He made only a few dollars a year. Along with his wages he received a blanket, one shirt, a pair of trousers, and a bit of tobacco. He carried a brightly painted paddle that indicated he was a "pork-eater," the group of paddlers who traveled each year between Montreal and Grand Portage at the western end of the Great Lakes.

For the twelve-hundred-mile journey from Montreal to Grand Portage, a voyageur's daily ration included a pound of dried corn, a strip of pork fat—from which his "pork-eater" name was derived—and an occasional cup of rum. He paddled for seven weeks, working fifteen to eighteen hours a day.

The voyageurs who worked at inland fur posts were called North men or

Portaging

River rapids and falls forced the voyageurs to unload their canoes and haul them and all the freight overland. Portages varied in length from a few feet to many miles, and they occurred often. In the first half of the journey from Lachine to Grand Portage, there were thirty-six portages and mini-portages, which required only partial unloading of the canoes.

Each package, or piece, was made up to weigh ninety pounds, and a voyageur carried two of these at a time with the help of a three-inch-wide leather strap called a portage collar. Smaller straps attached to the collar were first tied around a piece, which the voyageur swung onto his lower back. He then pulled the collar onto the top of his head so his head and neck could help support the load. With the collar in place, he grasped a second piece and laid it on top of the first. Leaning a little forward, the voyageur trotted the towering load, weighing more than he did, to the first stop of the portage. He quickly unloaded the packs and returned to the brigade's stopping place to repeat the task until all of the cargo and the canoe were about one-third of a mile along the trail. He and his colleagues continued to repeat this process until they reached the end of the portage.

Axheads threaded on ropes were slung around the voyageurs' necks, dangling like clunky necklaces. Gun crates, affectionately called "the dead" by the voyageurs because they were shaped like coffins, were the most miserable pieces to portage. One historian wrote that the awkward boxes rested "on the Packers rump and back of the head and in stepping over a log would by the lower part touching the log give the poor devil a rap on the head. ..."

TOP Artist Dennis Gale painted this watercolor of a canoe being carried across a Canadian portage.

ABOVE Artist Peter Rindisbacher traveled with a group of Hudson's Bay Company traders from York Factory to southern Manitoba in 1821. From that experience he created this watercolor painting titled Extremely Wearisome Journeys at the Portages.

winterers. They usually paddled smaller canoes back and forth from Grand Portage to wintering posts far into the Northwest and were considered more experienced and tougher than the pork-eaters.

In the two hundred years since Champlain had first rode a birchbark canoe into Lake Champlain with his Huron friends, the fur trade had developed into a business revolving around three groups of people: the traders and merchants, the voyageurs, and the Indians. At the top of the North West Company were traders and merchants like Alexander Henry, Peter Pond, Alexander Mackenzie, and Simon McTavish. As the trade grew, they replaced the independent traders, or woods runners, from a century before.

The Montreal agents who held the controlling interest in the North West Company arranged for the importing and transporting of trade goods and for the marketing of the furs. The wintering partners commanded the inland departments, or trading centers, along with distant trading posts. The clerks kept the records and managed the smaller posts. Together they were called the *bourgeois* by the Canadians.

The voyageurs were the truckers of the fur trade. Where a voyageur sat in his canoe indicated his position in the chain of command of the company. Captaining the canoe was the bowman, who sat in the front; second was the steersman, whose long, rudder-like paddle helped steer the canoe from the back; and the lowest positions were held by the middlemen, who sat in the middle of the canoe. The highest voyageur rank of all was the guide, who headed the brigade from the lead canoe.

Each spring shortly after the last flows of ice cleared the St. Lawrence, most of the citizens of Montreal trekked upriver a few miles to watch the first canoe brigades set out for the Northwest from Lachine, the little village founded by La Salle one hundred years earlier. The town was located just above a series of impassable river rapids. So starting from there ensured that the brigades would have smooth paddling for the first leg of their journey west.

The voyageurs were quite a sight. "One man's face … seemed to have been squeezed in a vice, or to have passed through a flattening machine. It was like a cheese-cutter,—all edge," described Dr. John J. Bigsby, who traveled with one of the brigades. "Another had one nostril bitten off. … A third man had his features wrenched to the right. … He had been slapped on the face by a grisly bear. Another was a short, paunchy old man, with vast features, but no forehead—the last man I should have selected. … he had been everywhere, and was famous for the weight of fish he could devour at a meal."

As the voyageurs went about loading the canoes and as families bunched together saying their good-byes, the traders of the North West Company arrived by carriage, accompanied by friends who came to see them off. After an elaborate farewell feast of sturgeon, venison, bear steaks, cheese, and great quantities of wine, the traders saw to the final loading of the huge canoes.

Stretching to nearly forty feet in length, these newly made Montreals, as the canoes were called, were six feet wide. Most of them were made in Three Rivers, a village on the St. Lawrence about ninety miles from Montreal. Kegs, wooden boxes called cassettes, bundles, bags—soon every canoe was filled to the gunwales with trade goods and supplies, including "sixty-five packages of goods, six hundred weight of biscuit, two hundred weight of pork, three bushels of pease, for the men's provision;" Mackenzie wrote. "Two oil cloths to cover the goods, a sail, &c. an axe, a towing-line, a kettle, and a sponge to bail out the water, with a quantity of gum, bark, and watape [spruce root], to repair the vessel. An European on seeing one of these slender vessels thus laden, heaped up, and sunk with her gunwale within six inches of the water, would think his fate inevitable in such a boat. …" In all, the canoes carried five thousand pounds of cargo each.

This sketch of a voyageur by C. S. Reinhart first appeared in Harper's Weekly. *It shows his ever-present pipe and woolen cap.*

Finally, with every piece packed and every voyageur in his proper position, the trader set his company flag in place at the stern of the canoe. Wives and children, parents, girlfriends, merchants, and clerks shouted and waved their good-byes. When someone on the bank fired a pistol, every paddle sliced into the icy water. Paddling forty to sixty strokes per minute, the brigade reached the center of the river

This lithograph of voyageurs walking a canoe up a rapid was created by British artist William Henry Bartlett, who visited Canada in the 1830s. The print appeared in Canadian Scenery, a book published in London in 1840.

in the time it took for the families to retreat from the docks for a clearer view of the departure. Seven weeks of adventure and grueling work lay ahead.

Only fifteen miles west of Lachine, the voyageurs landed so they could pray at the tiny stone church of St. Anne. Located at the northwest tip of Montreal Island, it was the first stopping point on the long trip. Each voyageur dropped a coin in the offering box and stepped inside the chapel to ask a blessing of their patron, St. Anne. Peter Pond wrote about the little church in his fancifully spelled narrative:

"thare Stans a Small Roman Church Aganst a Small Rapead this Church is Dedacateed to St Ann who Protescts all Voigeers."

Farther along, rowdy "baptisms" took place for new voyageurs on their first trip west. They involved a little dousing of water and more than a little consumption of rum. At the entry to every new river, the voyageurs doffed their caps and prayed. And at Georgian Bay, they tossed a trinket or pinch of tobacco overboard to appease the wind, which they called the "Old Woman."

On early spring mornings during the first leg of the trip, the voyageurs often had to break ice at the river's edge. But no matter how frigid the water, when rapids forced the brigade to stop or when the men paused for meals, the bowman jumped into the stream to steady the canoe, followed by the steersman and then the middlemen. To reach the shore with dry boots, the traders and their clerks rode piggyback or on the shoulders of the voyageurs.

The birchbark brigades poled and paddled their way up a series of Canadian rivers that included countless portages around long stretches of rapids and white water. Day and night mosquitoes and black flies swarmed in clouds about the workers' heads. Horseflies the size of bumblebees buzzed in dizzying circles. The voyageur's choice of repellent, bear grease and skunk oil, along with infrequent bathing gave him a distinct odor.

In his book Minnesota and the Far West *published in 1855, British travel writer Laurence Oliphant describes in detail his canoe journey across northern Minnesota. This illustration shows he and his travel companions smoking their pipes while "gliding easily and rapidly down the stream."*

Each day of the trip west started long before dawn when the guide roused the men from their blankets on the rocky shoreline. They paddled two or three hours before stopping for breakfast. Every meal was the same. A large tin kettle brimming with ten gallons of water was hung over a fire. A measure of peas or cornmeal—one quart per man—was poured in along with two or three pounds of pork fat cut into strips. The kettle bubbled and boiled until it was so thick you could stand a stick straight up in it. Then the hungry men squatted in a circle around the pot and, dipping their wooden spoons into it, they downed the whole mess in nothing flat.

Other than breakfast and the midday meal, rests occurred only when the trader called for a pipe. For a few brief moments, the men laid down their paddles and lit up their pipes. Each day's trip was measured by the number of pipes smoked.

TOP *Canadian painter Frances Anne Hopkins accompanied her husband, a Hudson's Bay Company official, on extended trips along some of the most important fur-trading routes in North America. This painting,* Canoe Manned by Voyageurs Passing a Waterfall, *is from a trip in 1869.*

ABOVE *Frances Anne Hopkins's images from her Lake Superior trip in 1869 capture some of the ever-present conditions on that dangerous and unpredictable lake.*

Several weeks into the trip, Lake Superior—the largest freshwater lake in the world—loomed just ahead. Superior's frigid water and huge waves made it the most dangerous part of the journey. The canoe brigades held close to the shore. In some places, sheer rocky cliffs resembling great slabs of cast iron rose straight up out of the water, making it impossible to find safe harbor from a storm. The big lake was notorious for its unpredictable storms and confusing fog.

When fifteen-year-old George Nelson, a newly hired clerk, first set eyes on Lake Superior, he wrote, "I was much surprised, & gazed with delight & amazement, at the immense expanse of water to the West. … It was awful to behold the immense size of the waves. — They were so large that when on their top we seemed as if going into an abyss, & we would drive down as from the top of a high hill & wanted to run through the one before us." Just when the canoe rushed down one of those waves, the steersman in Nelson's canoe reached for a handful of corn and ended upside down in the bottom of the canoe. Young Nelson couldn't contain his laughter.

If caught in a big storm, finding shelter was a matter of life and death. If not maneuvered expertly, the fragile canoes could crumple in huge lake swells or among the rocks and shoals. Like most people of the eighteenth century, voyageurs couldn't swim. If a man fell overboard in the icy-cold water, he often died.

Sometimes storms drenched the men and their cargo, forcing them to go ashore and dry everything out. Lengths of calico lay on bushes, and blankets hung from trees. When they finally were underway again, they had to paddle even faster and for longer hours to make up for lost time. At other times, the lake winds blew gently from behind and the sails were raised. The voyageurs sat back, puffed on their pipes, and enjoyed the ride.

When the brigade sighted the Suzie Islands, a smattering of tiny wooded islets a short distance from Grand Portage, they knew the trip was nearly over. On a spit of sandy beach, the canoes stopped long enough for the voyageurs to clean up, shave, and put on their best shirts and sashes. A few tucked ostrich plumes in their caps while the traders pulled their best tall beaver hats from their cassettes and donned their frock coats.

The voyageurs' voices floated in rhythmic melody across the smooth

In this well-known Frances Anne Hopkins painting from 1879, the danger and effort of paddling a huge Montreal canoe is evident.

This photo of a Métis family was taken in the early 1900s. Métis, which means "mixed blood," are Canadian families descended from marriages between Indians in fur country and the French, English, or Scottish traders.

Métis

Many voyageurs decided not to return to Montreal when their contracts expired and remained in the Northwest as "free" Canadians. Through intermarriage with the Indians, they created another group called the métis. Free Canadians and métis often provided contract labor at the trading posts and became an important cultural group within the trade.

expanse of Grand Portage Bay. Most of the songs told of lost love, included lots of repetition, and had several verses. One of the voyageurs' favorites was *À La Claire Fontaine*, a simple folk song sung coast to coast wherever there were voyageurs. It had nearly a dozen verses. The first is translated here:

At the clear running fountain
Sauntering by one day,
I found it so compelling
I bathed without delay.
Your love long since overcame me,
Ever in my heart you'll stay.

It was an adventurous life, glorified in tall tales and endless songs. One old paddler, past the age of seventy, bragged, "I could carry, paddle, walk and sing with any man I ever saw. ... I pushed on—over rapeds, over cascades, over chutes; all were the same to me. No water, no weather ever stopped the paddle or the song. ... There is no life so happy as a voyageur's life."

At this point in the journey, with their destination in sight, most of the voyageurs would probably have agreed with the old man's romantic memory of life in the fur trade. As they rounded Hat Point, their birchbark canoes cut through the glassy waters of Grand Portage Bay, creating a fan-shaped wake behind them. Finally their huge canoes and valuable cargo had reached the geographical heart of the fur trade.

CHAPTER 9

"A Famous Ball in the Dining Room"

An echoing boom from the cannon and a volley of musket fire from the stockade surrounding the post heralded the appearance of another brigade. In 1799, when Simon McTavish arrived at Grand Portage for the North West Company's annual rendezvous, or meeting, the fur post on the north shore of Lake Superior was the center of trade in North America. The place was huge and nearly bursting with people.

A palisade built of fifteen-foot-tall cedar posts began barely twenty paces from the water. The wall, with its jagged-tooth top and sentry buildings at the corners, gave the whole place a military air. But no one ever expected the post to be attacked—especially by Indians, who were welcomed inside as important customers. The palisade helped control traffic, protected the valuable trade goods from thieves, and helped keep the voyageurs' rowdy activities under control.

In 1936, an archaeological investigation of the Grand Portage fur-trade depot was begun, and trenches where the original stockade had stood were discovered. Two years later, the palisade of cedar posts was erected and then replaced in the 1960s as the Grand Portage National Monument reconstruction got underway.

The smell of cook fires and drying fish wafted through the air. The rough-sawn wooden buildings were roofed with cedar shingles. The doors and windows were painted brown. The guardhouses were manned around the clock chiefly to watch for and prevent fires from starting within the post's sixteen buildings. One errant spark landing on a wooden roof could send the entire post up in flames.

The warehouses, where bales of fur from the interior and trade goods from Montreal were processed, lined one side of the compound. Each bundle with its original weight marked on it was reweighed to make sure nothing was missing.

Then the pieces were unpacked and sorted to fill trade-good orders from the wintering partners.

Harried clerks and laborers scrambled to fill all the orders. As piles of blankets, kegs of liquor, and bolts of calico were divvied out and assembled for each trader, the orders were carefully tabulated so charges were recorded fairly. The weight of each keg and pack was marked on the parcel, and the North West Company logo, *NW*, was stamped in black ink before the pieces were hauled up the Grand Portage trail.

The portage itself was an eight-and-a-half-mile-long hilly, rock-strewn path from the post on Lake Superior northwest to Fort Charlotte, a dismal cluster of fly-infested log shacks on the Pigeon River. As the receiving station for the furs brought in from trading posts all across the Northwest, Fort Charlotte bustled with activity in July. Packs of furs that arrived daily needed to be transported to the post and packs of trade goods needed to be hauled up the trail and loaded into canoes bound for the interior. In the contract each voyageur signed in Montreal, he had agreed to lug eight packs across the portage before he could join the rendezvous at the fur post.

The steamy heat of early July made the job nearly unbearable. With 180 pounds balanced on his back, a cloud of mosquitoes and black flies whining in his ears, and visions of the festivities at Grand Portage in his exhausted brain, the newly arrived voyageur trotted a half mile up one of the longest portages in North America, rested

briefly, and then returned to bring another load to the first stop. Every keg and cassette was hauled to one stop before any were carried to the next. Finally after sixteen stops, he reached the bank of the Pigeon River, nearly nine miles inland. There he swung two 90-pound packs of furs onto his back and retraced his steps. For each additional pack carried beyond the eight required by his contract, the voyageur received a Spanish dollar, a valuable payment.

A constant stream of men shuttled back and forth over the portage, hauling supplies to the Northwest one way and furs from the Northwest the other way. To relieve the drudgery, the men tried

By the time Grand Portage was the center of the fur trade, the Spanish dollar, or "piece of eight," was used widely in Europe, the Americas, and Asia and had become the first world currency. It was legal tender in the United States until 1857.

to outdo each other, taunting and cursing at each other's clumsiness or lack of speed.

The North men—voyageurs who had spent the preceding winter trading with the Indians hundreds of miles inland—strolled past the trudging, bent-over pork-eaters. North men hiked the portage only once with their personal belongings, a clear sign of their higher standing with the North West Company.

When the North men arrived at the fort, they surged into the stockade, eager for the feast of bread and butter, pork, and the extra cup of rum each man received at the end of the journey. They hadn't tasted a bite of bread since leaving Grand Portage at the end of last year's rendezvous. They were starved for something other than pemmican and fish.

Frances Anne Hopkins painted Canoe Party Around Campfire *from a sketch she made in 1870 while traveling with her husband on the North American fur-trade routes.*

They also hungered for news and camaraderie. After stuffing themselves at the feast and hearing messages from their family and friends, they spent hours sharing stories and basking in the company of other winterers. As the sun faded behind the hills to the west, they found it hard to tear themselves from the friendly group and set up their tents south of the post.

When the pork-eaters finally settled in, it was beneath their upturned canoes on the north side of the palisade. Fights between the pork-eaters and the North men were frequent and often made worse by too much drinking.

As more and more brigades arrived from the interior, the trade goods in the storerooms moved out and smelly bales of furs moved in. The pelts were hurriedly inspected and repacked. Time was short. If the North men were delayed on their return trip to the interior, the lakes and rivers could freeze up before they reached their destinations.

In the counting house, tall wooden writing desks held thick ledgers filled with the spidery scribbles of clerks who entered each transaction at values figured in beaver skins. The prices of all the trader's goods were calculated based on a unit of value equal to one good beaver skin. A large blanket was worth five skins. A yard of calico was worth one skin. Twenty-five sewing needles were worth one skin. An ax was worth two.

George Nelson described his activities at Grand Portage during the rendezvous: "I was placed in one of the Stores to Serve the people. At last they began to come in. All was business. Receiving Goods, corn, flour, pork &c. &c. from Montreal & Mackinac, & furs from the different wintering posts,—Gambling, feasting, dancing, drinking & fighting."

Each passing July day brought new brigades from the north with more wintering partners and more bales of fur. While thousands of bales, kegs, and

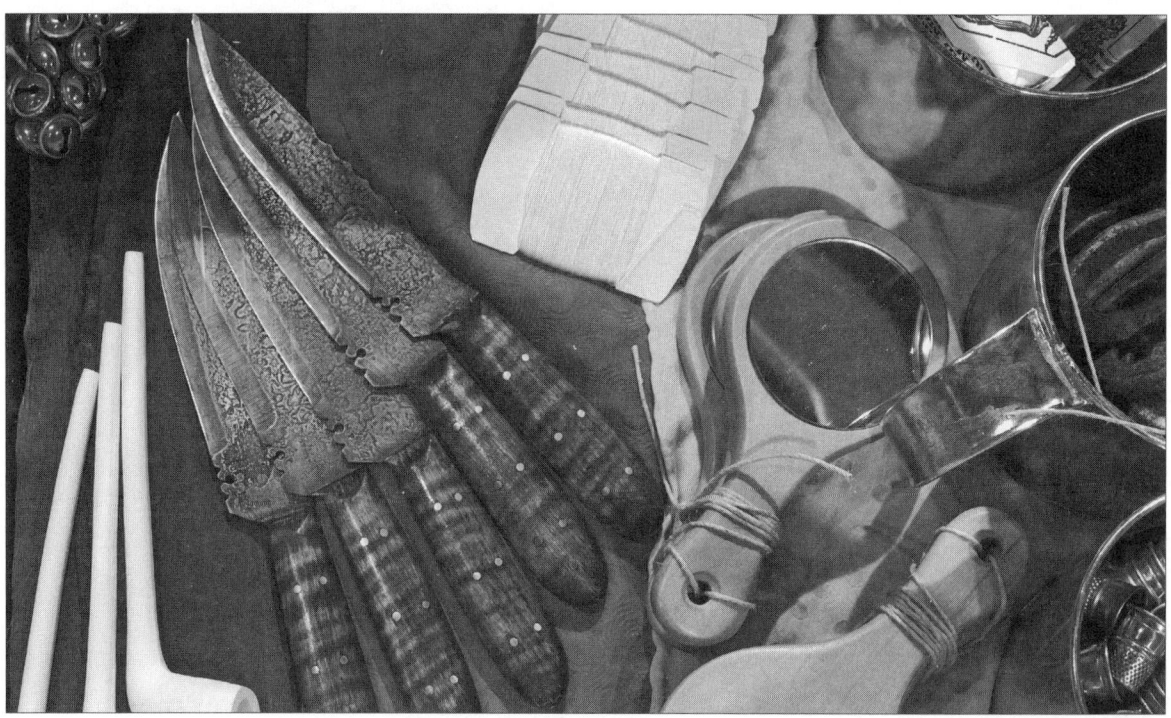

Common trade goods such as clay pipes, knives, thread, small mirrors, and thimbles were packed in bundles and boxes and carried to the interior by the traders.

cassettes piled up in the warehouses and were repacked, McTavish and the other partners of the North West Company convened their annual meeting. They probably met in the Great Hall. The stately room with eastern windows looking out on the brilliant waters of Lake Superior resembled a large colonial meeting hall where several hundred could gather. The windows were framed in brown trim, and from the whitewashed ceiling hung wrought-iron chandeliers filled with dozens of candles. All of it had arrived via canoe. No roads led to Grand Portage.

At the annual meeting, the partners voted to distribute the year's earnings and consider who should be allowed shares in the company. The original partners in the North West Company had been business associates in Montreal. At first there had been sixteen shares in the company divided among the winterers and the Montreal merchants. But each time the group met at Grand Portage, they gathered more competitors into the fold and by 1799 there were nearly a hundred shares. They called each trading year an "adventure," and the accounts for each shareholder had to be kept separate because the company reorganized almost every year.

In 1799, the company employed 50 clerks, 71 interpreter-clerks, 35 guides, and 1,120 canoemen, and McTavish managed it all with an iron hand. He believed in centralized control of the business, much to the frustration of the wintering partners, who had less and less input on the quality of the trade goods they received and little to say about how things were being run. They thought McTavish treated them like hired hands instead of partners. The year before, several unhappy wintering partners had decided to form their own company, which they named the XY Company.

But the North West Company's success was so ensured that the partners never considered failure, even in the face of close competition. None of the profits were put back into the company, and no reserve fund existed. They had united the best fur traders in the world, and their success in pushing farther and farther into the Northwest brought greater and greater profits. Many had already built lavish mansions in Montreal.

The rendezvous continued through most of July. In the evenings, the smell of roasted hams, venison, and beef drifted from the kitchens, located directly behind

The XY Company and Alexander Mackenzie

The XY Company, a short-lived competitor of the North West Company, was started in 1798 by a group of men who were unhappy with Simon McTavish's leadership. It was in direct and intense competition with the North West Company. The new group had originally called itself the New North West Company but shortened the name to XY for the two letters that follow W in the alphabet.

In 1802, Alexander Mackenzie gained control of the XY Company. The legendary trader and explorer had left the North West Company two years earlier after a power struggle with Simon McTavish at Grand Portage. Following the disagreement, the partners voted not to renew his share. He then sailed to England, where he was treated as a colonial hero and a celebrity. While there, Mackenzie published his maps and memoirs of his cross-continental adventure to such exceptional interest that the king made him a knight.

When he returned to Canada with a considerable fortune gained from his book, he decided to sign on with the XY Company. Lingering resentment over the feud with McTavish and his nephews made Mackenzie hungry for revenge. The new company with "The Knight" as its head was a tough competitor, but the XY Company took an unexpected turn. In 1804, Simon McTavish died suddenly of complications from a cold he caught while supervising the construction of his new mansion in Montreal. At that point, McTavish's successor asked the traders of the XY to join the North West Company, which they did.

the Great Hall. When the dinner bell rang, crowds of men moved in to find their places at one of the long tables. Only the higher-ranking members of the fur trade were allowed to eat here. Newly arrived wintering partners especially looked forward to crusty loaves and fresh butter.

The white tablecloths, glowing pewter flatware, and sparkling china and glassware from England made the banquet tables appear fit for royalty. The meals were formal. Everyone stood at his chair until the company partners entered dressed in their finest coats, breeches, and silk vests. All were seated according to rank, and when the feasting finally began in earnest, great platters of meat, fresh vegetables, and "tea, spirits, wine, &c. and plenty of milk" were served.

Following the meal, the lower ranks were dismissed and the partners continued discussing business and planning for the coming season. But one night in mid-July was reserved for the annual North West Ball. Everyone left the hall after dinner to prepare for it.

"This evening the Gentlemen of the place dressed & we had a famous Ball in the Dining Room … ," wrote one clerk. "For musick we had the Bag-Pipe the Violin, the Flute & the Fife, which enabled us to spend the evening agreeably."

Banquet tables ready for "the famous ball in the dining room" are apparent in this contemporary photo of the restored Great Hall at Grand Portage National Monument in northern Minnesota.

Agents, partners, clerks, interpreters, guides, and the Indian wives and daughters of the traders streamed into the Great Hall dressed in their finest. The ball was the social highlight of the season, and everyone danced until dawn. A few short hours later, bleary-eyed clerks returned to their books and bundles. Most of the fort went back to work, and the first groups of winterers prepared to head up the Grand Portage trail to the staging docks at Fort Charlotte.

The wintering North men would soon begin the long journey inland and build trading posts to protect all the goods they had brought back to trade with the Indians. As they tucked the last of their supplies and food into the canoes, each winterer anticipated a wilderness year of adventure and profit. Many had no idea of the struggles they would encounter.

CHAPTER 10

"We Did Not Make Palaces"

In the hot days of late July, brigades of North canoes were timed to leave the docks at Fort Charlotte on the far end of the Grand Portage every two days. That schedule helped to prevent canoe traffic jams at inland portages. If more than one brigade traveled over a portage at the same time, cargo inevitably got mixed up or left behind, and the whole effort became a logistical mess.

A North canoe was smaller and lighter than the huge, awkward Montreals, allowing it to move easily along the smaller rivers beyond Grand Portage. Each canoe could hold about half the amount of the larger vessel and, when empty, could be carried over a portage by two men. Six to eight voyageurs paddled each North canoe and traveled in smaller brigades of four or five. But occasionally, only two or three canoes headed for an inland post. That was the case for George Nelson.

He was homesick even before his brigade left Montreal in the spring of 1802. Three months before his sixteenth birthday, George Nelson signed a contract with the XY Company to serve as a clerk at a wintering fur post somewhere beyond Grand Portage.

Nelson was the oldest of eight children and had been well educated by his schoolmaster father. The family had settled in a small town near Montreal after leaving New York during the American Revolution. The fur trade was a big part of life on the St. Lawrence River, and Nelson wanted to be part of the adventure. Because he could read and write, he was offered a five-year contract as an apprentice clerk. He would receive a salary of fifteen pounds a year (approximately twenty-five dollars) and an opportunity to one day become a shareholder in the company.

Nelson's journals describe his adventures during his first years in the fur trade. "This far," he wrote, "every thing was new & strange to me; wild, romantic & wonderful. No 'falls' ... but many rapids, at several of which many a poor canadian found his watery grave. Portages over rocks, hills & Swamps, mostly covered with dense forests. Not a few of them the theme of legends, stories & tales of adventures, accidents & miracles &c. &c. "

Nelson's Montreal-to-Grand-Portage trip grew long and the food was dull. At one point he wrote, "indian corn was served out to the men for their rashions. … This was *all* they had except some 'grease', tallow, to season it with."

When the brigade finally reached Grand Portage, Nelson was placed in one of the stores to serve the traders as they arrived from the interior. The conflicts between the North West Company and the XY Company escalated and tempers flared. As Nelson and the three voyageurs assigned to him—all former employees of the North West Company—prepared to leave for their wintering camp, they were confronted about changing allegiance. "We were at dinner," Nelson wrote. "The men came running up saying Mr. McGillivray was going to carry off [our] men by main force. 'The Knight' [Mackenzie] ran down, we all followed. And no small affair it was. All in words, menaces & gestures indeed, but these are often the fore-runners of blood. We at last embarked fully determined to defend ourselves, fight, & kill, if driven too it; & armed for the purpose."

One can only imagine Nelson, the homesick schoolboy, attempting to defend the voyageurs. Fortunately, all was resolved, and before long Nelson and his three veteran winterers set out for the "Folle-avoine," or wild-rice region, in what is now northern Wisconsin.

"It was of a Wednesday, the 13" Sept. 1802, I was shipped off on board a Canoe, with Three men, to winter & trade amongst a tribe of indians remarkable for their courage," he wrote. He missed his family. "I shall never forget this first night I slept alone in my tent … my poor little heart was near bursting with fear, anxiety & grief."

Nelson's three companions were older and much more experienced. As the post clerk and the only one of them who could read or write, Nelson was expected to be in charge. Constant squabbles erupted as the men

Wild rice is native to the Great Lakes region and parts of Canada, and was an essential food for the traders. When boiled slowly for three or four hours, it turned into a kind of mush that could be seasoned with grease and sometimes maple sugar.

George Nelson and his voyageurs took several days to decide where to construct their log buildings. Enough clay had to be available so they could plaster their chimneys and chink the spaces between the logs of their cabins.

jockeyed for control of the group. At one point early in their journey to the inland post, one of the three shot a duck for dinner. Nelson was already tired of corn and looked forward to a good meal. But when the voyageur singed the duck on the fire, split it open, and tossed it into the pot of boiling corn without even washing it, Nelson was aghast. "O, what a barbarian! what a hog! am I to become like these!" The older voyageurs probably loved horrifying the greenhorn.

Finally after several weeks, which included a stop while an Ojibwa family made them another canoe, the winterers arrived at Yellow Lake in northwestern Wisconsin. "The indian name is 'Yellow water lake' from the yellow sand in the bottom," he wrote. "An immense quantity of rice grows there; and in their Season, ducks of various Sorts, Geese & Swans in multitudes. There is also plenty of fish."

Nelson and his XY Company voyageurs decided to build their winter quarters only ninety-five feet from the North West Company post on the Yellow River. Everyone involved in the fur trade knew that the Folle-avoine region of Wisconsin was on the northern edge of a war zone. Bands of Dakota held lands to the south and southwest and fought to maintain their hunting areas against Ojibwa encroachment. Because the contested area was rich in valued animals such as black bear, beaver, and white-tailed deer, it was considered a profitable but dangerous hunting ground. So concerned traders from rival companies occasionally built posts right next to each other for safety.

As the fall days grew shorter and cooler, Nelson wrote a detailed description of the log buildings he and his voyageurs built. "We did not make *palaces*," he observed. They cut the logs the length required for the house and stacked them one on top of the other to about five feet high with two stakes at each end to prevent the wall from falling. "The whole is plaistered [plastered], & upon the roof a layer of long Grass & a few inches of earth upon this to prevent the wind carrying it off."

Nelson recalled in a journal he wrote thirty years later: "Such was the method, my first years, of *Building.* an axe to each man, with a hoe that served as occasion

Although beaver pelts were the main furs acquired from the Indians, other furs such as fox, mink, and ermine were also obtained.

Trade silver consisted of sterling silver brooches, rings, and earrings, which were available at the fur posts. Artist Paul Kane painted this image of Ke-wah-ten, or the "North Wind," a member of the Menomonee tribe, wearing a dazzling array of trade silver.

might require, for an adze [an ax-like tool for trimming and smoothing wood], 25 nails for the Door & window & sometimes an augur, completed the amount of our tools!"

With only a sack of flour, a couple of pounds of tea and coffee, a little sugar, and salt to see them through the harsh winter, the traders depended completely on the Ojibwa to supplement their food supply. Nelson and his men traded for venison, fish, and, most of all, wild rice. The rice was boiled or fried until it burst like popcorn and was usually mixed with some sort of fat. Nelson noted how much wild rice each man received a day: "The allowance is one quart, with two ounces of grease, (when we have it) to season it, to each man."

The winter passed much like it did in all the posts across the interior. Local Ojibwa Indians brought in beaver pelts and other furs. The dried pelts were packed in a fur press and then wrapped with fabric into ninety-pound bales.

A store of trade goods was set up in one of the log rooms of the compound. Ojibwa women chose beads, cloth, and awls from the assortment of goods displayed. Trade silver such as brooches, rings, earrings, and bracelets glowed next to the blankets, axes, guns, and gunpowder. Small casks of high wine, a concentrated liquor that was watered down and traded, rounded out the selection of goods available from Nelson's store.

George Nelson was amazed at his surroundings and the Indians he met. He wrote: "there is not, & cannot be a more happy race of men in the world. Independance absolute, rendering unto each his due, they are sure of their own. ... The old men told

Each fur post had a room set up as a store where trade goods were displayed. Indians from the area surrounding the post could visit and buy goods such as blankets, cloth, axheads, trade silver, and guns.

me that all was in common before we came in amongst them to put an imaginary value upon their furs. ... They consider every man equal, since every man comes into, & goes out of, the world in the same way. ... Their laws are few indeed & simple, *Do well to me & I will do well to you. ...*"

CHAPTER 11

"I Found a Piece of Stone"

By the time George Nelson and his burly voyageurs built their wintering post in northwest Wisconsin, the North American fur trade involved thousands of traders and voyageurs scattered from the St. Lawrence River to the Great Lakes and Upper Canada; from the Mississippi to the Missouri rivers and the western plains beyond.

When Lewis and Clark arrived in the Mandan villages of the upper Missouri River in the fall of 1804, the tribes already possessed European trade goods acquired decades before. The North West Company traders had been frequent visitors and winterers. The pemmican and wild game Lewis and Clark's Corps of Discovery survived on were provided by Indians well practiced in supplying traders.

In 1794, President George Washington sent John Jay to England to negotiate a treaty that would end border disputes between the United States and Britain's Canadian provinces. This is a painting of Jay when he was the first Chief Justice of the United States Supreme Court.

As each year passed in the fur-trading wilderness of North America, it became more difficult for traders and Indians to "do well" to each other—the phrase George Nelson wrote toward the end of his first year wintering in Wisconsin. In the years before the XY Company was formed, the North West Company had shipped an average of 9,600 gallons of liquor to the west each year. In 1803, the total nearly doubled. Seasoned traders observed that the North West Company had set the west awash in rum. Food became scarce as Indian hunters struggled to meet the traders' need for fresh game, and tribes began to compete for hunting and trapping territory.

More changes came when the United States finally decided to enforce Jay's Treaty, a 1794 agreement that required the British to withdraw from all the posts they occupied in the Northwest Territory and had promised to abandon. The treaty, negotiated by the United States' first chief justice, John Jay, went into effect in 1796 but it wasn't immediately enforced. The North West Company partners knew that their main post, Grand Portage, was on the American side of the border and were at a loss about what to do.

As the partners considered their Grand Portage problem, a new employee named David Thompson, who had formerly worked for the Hudson's Bay Company, joined the group. He was a brilliant surveyor and spent the next ten months locating the exact boundary between the two countries. Grand Portage was indeed on the American side of the border and would have to be abandoned. Luckily that same year, another trader overheard some local Indians talking about another way from Lake Superior into the interior. They pointed out the old route by the Kaministiquia River in Canada that the French had used before they were defeated in 1760. By 1800, the North West Company had men working to drain the swampy flat on the Kaministiquia where the new fur post would stand, and Simon McTavish immediately ordered that no time be lost in moving the location of the summer rendezvous.

The summer of 1802 was the last time Grand Portage served as the meeting place for the North West Company. The new sprawling complex on the shallow, narrow Kaministiquia River was named Fort William for William McGillivray, who had taken control of the company when his uncle Simon McTavish died.

When the War of 1812 between Great Britain and the United States broke out, it interrupted trade all across

TOP *David Thompson was considered one of history's greatest land geographers. He mapped well over a million square miles of North America. This is an artist's rendering of the famous explorer and fur trader. No known historic image of him exists.*

ABOVE *This was the hub of the North West Company's fur-trade empire once the business vacated Grand Portage in 1802. (It was later called Fort William.) Today the reconstructed heritage fort is located in Thunder Bay, Ontario.*

the continent. At one point during the war, American ships controlled Lake Erie and completely stopped all flow of goods in and out of fur country. The British blockade of the Atlantic coastline further strangled the movement of goods and furs.

Soon after that, Lord Selkirk, a Scotsman who had acquired a number of shares in the Hudson's Bay Company, was granted a huge tract of land right in the middle of the North West Company's prime fur-trading area in the Red River valley of what is now southern Manitoba. He was determined to colonize the region and turn it into farmland. Settlement had always been the death knell to the fur trade. A series of clashes led to armed war between the traders and Selkirk's colonists. The wilderness turned into a war zone.

The conflict weakened both companies. Along with fighting the Hudson's Bay Company, the North West Company found that trade in the far northern reaches of Canada was becoming prohibitively expensive and complicated because of the long distances traveled. The company began to go into debt.

In 1821, determined to end the conflict and to bring stability to the frontier, agents for the North West Company traveled to England to negotiate a settlement with the Hudson's Bay Company officials. In the end the two companies merged, and the North West Company was folded into the Hudson's Bay Company. By the time George Nelson retired from the trade in 1823—a bitter, discouraged man with few resources—all of its operations had moved north into Canada. Tiny outposts like the one he and his voyageurs built in 1802 were abandoned and eventually decayed to the point that only trained archaeologists could determine their locations.

Artist Peter Rindisbacher painted this watercolor of the Red River Settlement in the summer of 1822. The simple log house with a fenced-in garden sits on the bank of the river.

As the trade grew and changed, it

spawned a century of displacement and misery for the Indian tribes. American settlements disrupted trade routes and the Indians' nomadic way of life. The American Fur Company, started by John Jacob Astor to compete with the North West Company, became the most hated organization on the American frontier. Small traders were crushed, and Indians were plied with alcohol. Liquor became a currency of the trade. President Zachary Taylor considered American Fur's employees to be "the greatest scoundrels the world ever knew."

By the mid-1800s, the fur trade slowly began to collapse. It had functioned well when the Indians had controlled the land because they knew how to efficiently trap the beavers. But once they were pushed farther west and onto reservations, the business was ruined. As the fur-trade era faded, many traders entered new businesses of real estate, lumbering, mining, and railroading. Some continued to operate small stores.

The fur-trade boom finally ended when fashion changed. By the 1840s, beaver hats were considered old-fashioned. Paris hatters had designed a new hat of silk that was lightweight, elegant, and cheaper than the "beavers." In an ironic twist of

history, the silk originally sought from China by countless explorers replaced the North American beaver fur discovered while seeking China's silk.

By 1930, the fur trade was all but forgotten, even in places where it had once flourished. It was the Great Depression, and many people were out of work. Times were tough in Pine City, Minnesota, a small town along the Snake River in what had been wild-rice country a hundred years before.

Joe Neubauer, an eleven-year-old son of a blacksmith, spent countless afternoons in his father's shop, listening to the stories farmers told as they waited to have a plow repaired or a tool sharpened. They puffed on their pipes and talked of the Indians who had lived and traded along the river

When Joe Neubauer (left) was about nine years old, he posed with his brother, Albert, for this photo with their dog.

Fur trader John Jacob Astor began with a sack of trade goods on his back and ended up as the fourth-richest American to ever live, with an estimated estate in today's dollars of about $110 billion.

John Jacob Astor

About the time Alexander Mackenzie reached the Pacific Ocean and secured his name in history, John Jacob Astor was purchasing his first ships for the trade. A twenty-one-year-old butcher's son from Waldorf, Germany, Astor had landed in America just after the Revolutionary War with seven wooden flutes under his arm and twenty-five dollars in his pocket. He married an ambitious, business-minded woman named Sarah Todd, and the two of them set up shop in tiny New York City, where they sold musical instruments and bought furs. Within a few weeks of their marriage, Astor took a boat up the Hudson to try his hand at fur trading.

He trudged through western New York and Pennsylvania with a pack of trade goods on his back and an amazing ability to make the best deal. When he discovered that the Indian tribes of the area liked music, he took out a flute from his pack and played a few German folk tunes for them. In less than ten years, Astor owned a fleet of ships transporting furs to Europe and China. As his business grew, he created the American Fur Company to compete with the North West Company.

Eventually, Astor eased out of the fur-trade business and turned his sights on New York City real estate. Hopeful farmers had cleared large tracts of land on Manhattan Island only to discover that the soil was rocky and not very good for growing crops. Astor bought hundreds of acres of poor farmland that are now situated in the middle of the most populous city in the United States.

By the time of his death in 1848, Astor was the richest person in the United States, leaving an estimated twenty million dollars—a tremendous amount of money 150 years ago. And it all began with furs.

and of all the arrowheads they found in their plowed fields. Joe was fascinated. He began looking for Indian artifacts and soon came across his first arrowhead. "That was the beginning," he remembered.

During Christmas vacation that December, he fell and badly broke his arm. Friends and neighbors visited and gave him get-well gifts of a nickel or a dime. By spring, he had saved up enough money to buy a ten-dollar rowboat, which made his trips up the Snake River in search of arrowheads easier. On a sunny August morning in 1932, he and a friend landed his boat on the south side of the river about a mile from town. They scrambled up a piney sand ridge to a corn-field that had just been picked. "We walked the rows," he remembered, "and I found a piece of stone."

His father identified the relic as a gun-flint and thought it must have come from the fur post that was known to have been somewhere in the area. Several years earlier, a historian had discovered a frayed, dilapi-dated diary of a North West Company fur trader in a library. The trader's name was John Sayer, and he had wintered on the Snake River in east-central Minnesota in 1804–05. His journal described life at the North West Company wintering post in all its snowy detail. But where had his post stood?

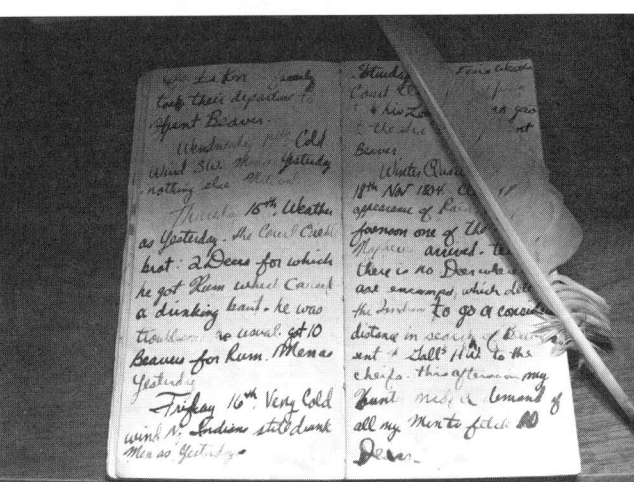

TOP A gunflint is a hard piece of stone or flint that provided the igniting spark in flintlock weapons of the eighteenth and nineteenth centuries. The one here is secured in a metal clamp located in the top center of the photograph.

ABOVE John Sayer's journal of his experiences at the North West Company Fur Post during the winter of 1804–05 describes the weather, post construction, and trade with the local tribes.

Joe Neubauer had found it. When the site was finally excavated by the Minnesota Historical Society in the 1960s, archaeologists painstakingly dug up and sifted through every inch of dirt until they discovered the exact location of the 1804 post. Over the next few years, they pieced together the construction details and convinced the state of Minnesota to fund the rebuilding of the fur post.

By the end of the decade, a palisade of one thousand tamarack trees cut from a nearby state forest and formed into posts surrounded a six-room log building. The entire structure was built exactly where it had stood a century and a half before. Schoolchildren, families, and tourists from all over the country visit the fort, a replica of an Ojibwa encampment, and an interpretive museum that dominates the ridge above the Snake River.

Joe Neubauer still lives in Pine City, a stone's throw from the North West Company Fur Post. He's in his eighties now and still remembers the stories his father told of the retired voyageurs who lived in the area. Joe's

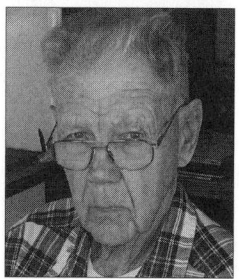

TOP Between 1965 and 1967, over thirty years after its original discovery, the North West Company Fur Post site was excavated by Hamline University students led by Dr. Leland Cooper. Hundreds of artifacts were recovered, including musket balls, gunflints, beads, knives, and axheads.

MIDDLE Surrounding the fur-post row house at the North West Company Fur Post at Pine City, Minnesota, is a palisade measuring 100 feet by 61 feet with defensive bastions in two of its corners.

BOTTOM Joe Neubauer, who is now in his eighties, still collects fur-trade artifacts similar to the ones he unearthed when he discovered the site of the North West Company Fur Post back in 1932.

grandfather made iron spearheads for the local Indians, and he remembers watching them harvest rice on the Snake River. Joe occasionally shares his extensive collection of axheads, musket balls, and gunflints stored in cigar boxes and on trays. Each year he attends the rendezvous held at the fort, where history buffs camp and reenact life during the fur-trade era.

Remnants of the fur trade are interwoven into all our lives. French place names like Duluth and Des Moines, New Orleans and Joliet come from the trade. River names like Mississippi, Ohio, and Missouri were first learned by the French and English from their Indian guides as they ventured west. Cities like

From 1968 to 1969, the North West Company Fur Post on the Snake River was reconstructed. It opened to the public in 1970 featuring a six-room row house measuring 77 feet long by 18 feet wide. Historical reenactors at the site bring the fur-trade era to life for visitors.

Albany, New York; Pittsburgh, Pennsylvania; Detroit, Michigan; Green Bay, Wisconsin; St. Louis, Missouri; and Cincinnati, Ohio, the site of Fort Washington in John Tanner's day, all began with the fur trade. For centuries it was the forerunner of settlement and the biggest business in North America.

The network of rivers, lakes, and streams that snakes across the continent like a huge circulatory system has shaped how our land was settled, how trade developed, and how transportation evolved. The birchbark brigades of canoes, traders, voyageurs, and Indians no longer travel through the interior. But people like Samuel de Champlain, Alexander Henry, Net-no-kwa and her son John Tanner, Alexander Mackenzie, George Nelson, and Joe Neubauer along with countless Indians and traders have all played a part in an old story that is still whispered in the piney treetops of the Northwest.

TIMELINE

1492	Italian explorer Christopher Columbus discovers the New World.
1497	English explorer John Cabot sails to North America and brings back accounts of incredibly abundant fisheries.
1500	European fishermen begin to make regular voyages to the fishing waters of the Grand Banks and subsequently trade for furs with the Indians they meet on the coast.
1534	French explorer Jacques Cartier and his men trade with Micmac Indians on the coast of New Brunswick, the first documented trading between Europeans and the inhabitants of the New World.
1598	French explorer Samuel de Champlain makes his first voyage to the New World.
1608	New France is founded by Champlain, who early on recognizes the importance of the fur trade to his colony.
1610	Champlain sends Étienne Brûlé to live with the Huron Indians and learn their languages and trade routes.
1610	English navigator Henry Hudson discovers Hudson Bay and is convinced it is the Northwest Passage to China. His crew mutinies and leaves him to die there while they return to England.
1618	Brûlé travels all the way to the eastern edge of Lake Superior in search of the Northwest Passage.
1630	The Iroquois tribes acquire guns from the Dutch traders and begin a ten-year assault on their French and Huron enemies, who control much of the fur trade.
1634	French explorer Jean Nicolet travels through the Great Lakes all the way to Green Bay and claims the entire region for France.
1659	French traders Pierre Esprit Radisson and Medard Seigneur Chouart des Grosseilliers make an unlicensed fur-trading excursion into the interior where they learn from the Indians of the abundant furs around Hudson Bay.
1670	The Hudson's Bay Company is chartered following Grosseilliers's successful trading voyage to the bay on the English ship the *Nonsuch*.

TIMELINE

1673	French explorers Jacques Marquette and Louis Joliet explore the Mississippi River as far as Arkansas and return to report of abundant furs available along that corridor.
1682	René-Robert Cavelier, Sieur de La Salle, and Louis Hennepin travel the Mississippi all the way to the Gulf of Mexico. They claim the entire watershed for France and name it Louisiana after King Louis XIV.
1701	The Great Peace is signed by the English, the French, and the various tribes of the Great Lakes, including thirty-nine chiefs. The treaty briefly ends decades of warfare between the Indians and the colonists.
1702–1713	Queen Anne's War is fought between England and Spain and between England and France for colonial territory.
1744–1748	France and Spain together fight England for land and power in North America.
1754	The French and Indian War begins. The fur trade is disrupted. Most of the licensed traders and their voyageurs are called east to fight the British.
1760	New France is conquered by the British. Furs now are shipped to London instead of Paris, and most trade goods are supplied through London.
1763	The Treaty of Paris formally ends the French and Indian War. France gives the British all of its land in North America east of the Mississippi River except for New Orleans. The French land west of the Mississippi, called Louisiana, is given to Spain.
Spring 1763	Pontiac's War begins when Ottawa war chief Pontiac, united with warriors from many Indian nations, attacks Fort Detroit. The uprising spreads throughout the region.
1765	Alexander Henry receives exclusive rights to trade on Lake Superior.
1767	British traders are allowed to establish wintering posts among the Indians. Construction of permanent structures at Grand Portage begins.

TIMELINE

1774	Traders begin to spread farther north and west of Grand Portage. Small partnerships are formed to battle the cut-throat competition between traders.
1776	The American Revolution causes some traders to avoid the areas south of the Great Lakes and encourages them to go farther north and west into what is today Manitoba, Saskatchewan, and Alberta.
1782	A smallpox epidemic kills thousands throughout the Northwest.
1784	The North West Company is formed. Sixteen company shares are held by traders and merchants such as Simon McTavish, Peter Pond, Alexander Henry, and three English brothers named Frobisher. Their first meeting is held at Grand Portage, which becomes the company's rendezvous point for the next twenty years.
1789	Alexander Mackenzie searches for the Northwest Passage but instead reaches the Arctic Ocean.
1793	Alexander Mackenzie successfully crosses the continent to the Pacific Ocean, just over three hundred years after Columbus first sailed west to find China. The route Mackenzie discovers is so difficult to traverse that it is seldom ever used.
1798	The rival XY Company is formed to compete with the North West Company.
1800	Alexander Mackenzie joins the XY Company.
1802	XY Company clerk George Nelson is sent into northern Wisconsin to build a wintering post. He keeps a journal of his experiences.
1803	The United States purchases the Louisiana territory from the French (The French had regained Louisiana in 1800.) The Lewis and Clark expedition heads west in search of a passage to the Pacific Coast.
1804	Simon McTavish, leader of the North West Company, dies, prompting the consolidation of the North West Company and the XY Company.

TIMELINE

1804   North West Company wintering partner John Sayer builds a trading post on the Snake River in east-central Minnesota and keeps a detailed journal of his experiences trading that year.

1808   The American Fur Company is formed by John Jacob Astor.

1812   The War of 1812 disrupts trade across the entire continent. At the war's end, the North West Company withdraws from American soil and operates only in Canada.

1821   The North West Company and the Hudson's Bay Company merge under the name Hudson's Bay Company.

1840s   Silk hats replace the beaver felt hats that have been in style for three hundred years. Beaver hats are now out of fashion in Europe, signaling the end of the fur-trade boom.

1932   Joe Neubauer finds a gunflint in a cornfield in east-central Minnesota. The site is later discovered to be the North West Company wintering post built by John Sayer and his voyageurs in 1804.

1960s   The Minnesota Historical Society begins excavating the site of the North West Company Fur Post on the Snake River in east-central Minnesota.

NOTES

Introduction   page 11

"hatchets, knives, scissors, needles …": Innes, Harold A. *The Fur Trade in Canada*, p. 110.

Chapter 1   page 15

"The Admiral bore the …": Medieval Source Book. "Christopher Columbus: Extracts from Journal," Fordham University Center for Medieval Studies, Internet Medieval Sourcebook. www.fordham.edu/halsall/source/columbus1.html.*

"found tall trees …": Croxton, Derek. "The Cabot Dilemma: John Cabot's 1497 Voyage and the Limits of Historiography." In *Essays in History*. Vol. 33. Charlottesville: University of Virginia, 1990–1991, p. 10. etext.lib.virginia.edu/journals/EH/EH33/croxto33.html.

"to hym that founde …": same as above.

"John [Cabot] set out in …": Vergil, Polydore. *The Anglica Historia of Polydore Vergil, A.D. 1485–1537*, p. 117. www.reformation.org/polydore-vergil.html.

"I am rather inclined …": Library and Archives of Canada. *Dictionary of Canadian Biography Online*. www.biographi.ca/009004-119.01-e.php?&id_nbr=107&interval=20&&PHPSESSID=ioli2p27bekjffamb925ltjgm1.

"brandishing peltry on sticks …": Wheeler, Robert C. *A Toast to the Fur Trade: A Picture Essay on Its Material Culture*, p. 4.

Chapter 2   page 26

"We heartily recommend …": Johansen, Bruce E. *Forgotten Founders: Benjamin Franklin, the Iroquois and the Rationale for the American Revolution*, chapter 4, page 5. www.ratical.org/many_worlds/6Nations/FF.html.

"which were as large …": Samuel de Champlain's *Voyages: Volume II, Part II*. Translated and transcribed for historiclakes.org. *The Journal of Samuel de Champlain*. www.historiclakes.org/S_de_Champ/Champlain2.html.

"We both began …": same as above.

"to inquire if they …": same as above.

"the entire night …": same as above.

"They came at a slow pace …": same as above.

"which astonished them anew …": same as above.

Chapter 3   page 36

"in their method of warfare …": Menard, Fr. Rene. "A Priest Journeys to a Wisconsin Village of Exiled Hurons in 1661." Wisconsin Historical Society, chapter 1. www.wisconsinhistory.org/turningpoints/search.asp?id=53.

"a great store of beaver …": Radisson, Pierre Esprit. *Voyages of Peter Esprit Radisson: Being an Account of His Travels and Experiences Among the North American Indians, From 1652 to 1684*. www.freeonlinebooks.org.

"He made my brother prisoner …": same as above.

"North West into …": Newman, Peter C. *Empire of the Bay*, p. 60.

*All Web sites active at time of publication

NOTES

Chapter 4   page 47

"I, René-Robert Cavelier de La Salle …": Virtual Museum of New-France: Cavelier de La Salle, p. 4. www.civilization.ca/cmc/index_e.aspx?ArticleID=3037.

"Should foreigners anticipate us …": Phillips, Paul Chrisler. *The Fur Trade.* Vol. 1, p. 237.

"My only reply …": Historica. History by the Minute. "Governor Frontenac." www.histori.ca/minutes/minute.do?id=10129.

Chapter 5   page 60

"They told me …": *George Washington's Journal,* 1753. Transcribed from the *Maryland Gazette,* March 21, 1754. Archiving Early America. www.earlyamerica.com./earlyamerica/milestones/journal/journaltext.html.

"Our horses were now so …": same as above.

"not 15 Steps …": same as above.

"Lands on the Ohio …": French and Indian War Commemoration. www.frenchandindianwar250.org.

"a volley fired by …": Walpole, Horace. www.frenchandindianwar250.org.

"Proposing to avail myself …": Henry, Alexander. *Travels and Adventures in Canada and the Indian Territories Between the Years 1760 and 1776,* p. 3.

"I was altogether a stranger …": same as above, p. 11.

"I had the satisfaction …": same as above, p. 35.

"At two o'clock …": same as above, p. 42.

"Englishman, you know …": same as above, pp. 43–45.

"that it was the good character …": same as above, pp. 46–47.

"furnish them …": same as above, p. 47.

Chapter 6   page 70

"he thought himself …": Wallace, W. Stewart. *The Pedlars from Quebec,* p. 21.

"found the traders …": Henry, Alexander. *Travels and Adventures in Canada and the Indian Territories: Between the Years 1760 and 1776,* p. 235.

"pent-up hornets' nest …": Gilman, Carolyn. *The Grand Portage Story,* p. 52.

"charming young man who loved …": Newman, Peter C. *Empire of the Bay: The Company of Adventurers That Seized a Continent,* p. 278.

"so light, that two men …": Mackenzie, Alexander. *The Journals of Alexander Mackenzie: Exploring Across Canada in 1789 and 1793,* p. 220.

"From these houses …": same as above, p. 364.

"I now mixed up …": Mackenzie, Alexander. *The Journals and Letters of Sir Alexander Mackenzie,* p. 378.

"Women employed all day …": Van Kirk, Sylvia. *Many Tender Ties.* From John Porter's Journal, 29; Hudson Bay Company's Archives.

"rounded a point …": Mackenzie, Alexander. *The Journals of Alexander Mackenzie: Exploring Across Canada in 1789 and 1793,* p. 407.

NOTES

Chapter 7   page 79

"that from the actions ...": Tanner, John. *The Falcon: A Narrative of the Captivity and Adventures of John Tanner*, p. 3.

"seized by both hands ...": same as above, p. 3.

"I had probably made ...": same as above, p. 5.

"My old Indian mother ...": same as above, p. 15.

"was then advanced ...": same as above, p. 15.

"had the direction in ...": same as above, p. 16.

"she always carried ...": same as above, p. 19.

"It is time ...": same as above, p. 17.

"I ran home ...": same as above, p. 18.

"I was endeavouring ...": same as above, pp. 223–224.

Chapter 8   page 86

"One man's face ...": Nute, Grace Lee. *The Voyageur*, pp. 15–16.

"sixty-five packages of goods ...": Mackenzie, Alexander. *The Journals of Alexander Mackenzie: Exploring Across Canada in 1789 and 1793*, p. 29.

"thare Stans a Small ...": Gates, Charles M., ed. *Five Fur Traders of the Northwest*, p. 30.

"gliding easily ...": Oliphant, Laurence. *Minnesota and the Far West*, p. 90.

"I was much surprised ...": Nelson, George. *My First Years in the Fur Trade: The Journals of 1802–1804*, p. 40.

"At the clear running fountain ...": Nute, Grace Lee. *The Voyageur*, p. 106.

"I could carry ...": All About Canoes. www.canoe.ca/AllAboutCanoes/canoe_quotes.html.

"on the Packers rump and back ...": Cowie, Isaac. *The Company of Adventurers: A Narrative of Seven Years in the Service of the Hudson's Bay Company During 1867–1874*, p. 229.

Chapter 9   page 95

"I was placed ...": Nelson, George. *My First Years in the Fur Trade: The Journals of 1802–1804*, p. 42.

"tea, spirits, wine ...": Mackenzie, Alexander. *The Journals and Letters of Sir Alexander Mackenzie*, p. 98.

"This evening the Gentlemen ...": Harmon, Daniel Williams. *Sixteen Years in the Indian Country: The Journal of Daniel Williams Harmon, 1800–1816*, p. 22.

NOTES

Chapter 10   page 102

"This far, every thing ...": Nelson, George. *My First Years in the Fur Trade: The Journals of 1802–1804*, p. 38.

"indian corn was served ...": same as above, p. 40.

"We were at dinner ...": same as above, p. 45.

"It was of ...": same as above, pp. 45–46.

"I shall never forget ...": same as above, p. 46.

"O, what a barbarian! ...": same as above, p. 47.

"The indian name is ...": same as above, pp. 55–56.

"We did not make ...": same as above, p. 58.

"The whole is plaistered ...": same as above, p. 59.

"Such was the method ...": same as above, p. 60.

"The allowance is ...": same as above, p. 56.

"there is not ...": same as above, p. 16.

Chapter 11   page 108

"the greatest scoundrels ...": Madsen, Axel. *John Jacob Astor: America's First Multimillionaire*, p. 4.

BIBLIOGRAPHY

Books

Adney, Edwin Tappan, and Howard I. Chapelle. *The Bark Canoes and Skin Boats of North America.* Washington, DC: Smithsonian Institution, 1964.

Birk, Douglas A. *John Sayer's Snake River Journal, 1804–1805.* Minneapolis: Institute for Minnesota Archaeology, 1989.

Birk, Douglas A. *The Messrs. Build Commodiously: A Guide to John Sayer's 1804–1805 North West Company Wintering Expedition to the Snake River.* Brainerd, MN: Evergreen Press, 2004.

Bolz, J. Arnold. *Portage into the Past: By Canoe Along the Minnesota-Ontario Boundary Waters.* Minneapolis: University of Minnesota Press, 1960.

Campbell, Marjorie Wilkins. *The North West Company.* New York: St. Martin's Press, 1957.

Campbell, Marjorie Wilkins. *The Nor'westers: The Fight for the Fur Trade.* Calgary, AB: Fifth House, 2002.

Cowie, Isaac. *The Company of Adventurers: A Narrative of Seven Years in the Service of the Hudson's Bay Company During 1867–1874.* Lincoln: University of Nebraska Press, 1993.

Dunn, James Taylor. *The St. Croix: Midwest Border River.* St. Paul: Minnesota Historical Society Press, 1979.

Gates, Charles M., ed. *Five Fur Traders of the Northwest.* St. Paul: Minnesota Historical Society Press, 1971.

Gilman, Carolyn. *The Grand Portage Story.* St. Paul: Minnesota Historical Society Press, 1992.

Gilman, Carolyn. *Where Two Worlds Meet: The Great Lakes Fur Trade.* St. Paul: Minnesota Historical Society Press, 1982.

Hanson, James A. *The Voyageur's Sketchbook.* Chadron, NE: The Fur Press, 1981.

Harmon, Daniel Williams. *Sixteen Years in the Indian Country: The Journal of Daniel Williams Harmon, 1800–1816.* Edited by W. Kaye Lamb. Toronto: Macmillan, 1957.

Henry, Alexander. *Travels and Adventures in Canada and the Indian Territories Between the Years 1760 and 1776.* Edited by James Bain. Rutland, VT: Charles E. Tuttle, 1969.

Huck, Barbara. *Exploring the Fur Trade Routes of North America.* Winnipeg, MB: Heartland, 2002.

Innis, Harold A. *The Fur Trade in Canada: An Introduction to Canadian Economic History.* Toronto: University of Toronto Press, 1999.

Johansen, Bruce E. *Forgotten Founders: Benjamin Franklin, the Iroquois and the Rationale for the American Revolution.* Ipswich, MA: Gambit, 1982.

Kalman, Bobbie, and Niki Walker. *Life in an Anishinabe Camp.* New York: Crabtree Publishing, 2003.

Lavender, David. *The Fist in the Wilderness.* Lincoln: University of Nebraska Press, 1964.

Mackenzie, Alexander. *The Journals and Letters of Sir Alexander Mackenzie.* Edited by W. Kaye Lamb. Cambridge: Cambridge University Press, 1970.

BIBLIOGRAPHY

Mackenzie, Alexander. *The Journals of Alexander Mackenzie: Exploring Across Canada in 1789 and 1793*. Santa Barbara, CA: Narrative Press, 2001.

Madsen, Axel. *John Jacob Astor: America's First Multimillionaire*. New York: John Wiley, 2001.

Nelson, George. *My First Years in the Fur Trade: The Journals of 1802–1804*. Edited by Laura Peers and Theresa M. Schenck. St. Paul: Minnesota Historical Society Press, 2002.

Newman, Peter C. *Empire of the Bay: The Company of Adventurers That Seized a Continent*. New York: Penguin Books, 2000.

Nute, Grace Lee. *The Voyageur*. St. Paul: Minnesota Historical Society Press, 1987.

Oliphant, Laurence. *Minnesota and the Far West*. Originally published in *Blackwood's Magazine*, London, 1855.

Phillips, Paul Chrisler. *The Fur Trade*. Vols. 1 and 2. Norman: University of Oklahoma Press, 1961.

Plummer-Steen, Mike. *The Grand Portage Guide*. Grand Portage, MN: Grand Portage National Monument, 2003.

Radisson, Pierre Esprit. *Voyages of Peter Esprit Radisson: Being an Account of His Travels and Experiences Among the North American Indians, From 1652 to 1684*. Gideon D. Scull, London, England, 1885. Publication of The Prince Society. Transcribed from original manuscripts in the Bodleian Library and the British Museum. www.freeonlinebooks.org.

Saum, Lewis O. *The Fur Trader and the Indian*. Seattle: University of Washington Press, 1965.

Sivertson, Howard. *The Illustrated Voyageur: Paintings and Companion Stories*. Mount Horeb, WI: Midwest Traditions, 1996.

Sonenscher, Michael. *The Hatters of Eighteenth-Century France*. Berkeley: University of California Press, 1987.

Tanner, John. *The Falcon: A Narrative of the Captivity and Adventures of John Tanner*. New York: Penguin Books, 1994.

Van Kirk, Sylvia. *Many Tender Ties: Women in Fur-Trade Society, 1670–1870*. Norman: University of Oklahoma Press, 1983.

Vennum, Thomas, Jr. *Wild Rice and the Ojibway People*. St. Paul: Minnesota Historical Society Press, 1988.

Vergil, Polydore. *The Anglica Historia of Polydore Vergil, A.D. 1485–1537*. Translated by Denys Hay. London: Office of the Royal Historical Society, 1950.

Wallace, W. Stewart. *The Pedlars from Quebec: And Other Papers on the Nor'westers*. Toronto: Ryerson Press, 1954.

Wheeler, Robert C. *A Toast to the Fur Trade: A Picture Essay on Its Material Culture*. St. Paul: Wheeler Productions, 1985.

BIBLIOGRAPHY

Anthologies

The World in 1492. New York: Henry Holt, 1992.

Web Sites*

CANADIANA.ORG
  www.canadiana.org/hbc/intro_e.html.
  The fur trade in Canada and how it led to the exploration of the country.

FRENCH AND INDIAN WAR COMMEMORATION
  www.frenchandindianwar250.org.
  Highlights all aspects of the French and Indian War.

HUDSON'S BAY COMPANY
  www.hbc.com/hbcheritage/history/overview.asp.
  Hudson's Bay Company history site.

HUDSON'S BAY COMPANY ARCHIVES
  www.gov.mb.ca/chc/archives/hbca.
  The Hudson's Bay Company's records document the history of the HBC since its inception in 1670, marking the history of the fur trade, North American exploration, the development of Canada as a country, and the growth of HBC's Canadian retail empire.

LIBRARY AND ARCHIVES CANADA
  www.collectionscanada.ca/index-e.html.
  Canada's national collection of books, historical documents, government records, photos, films, maps, music, and more.

MINNESOTA HISTORICAL SOCIETY
  www.mnhs.org/places/sites/nwcfp.
  Minnesota Historical Society's North West Company Fur Post site.

THE MOUNTAIN MAN PLAINS INDIAN CANADIAN FUR TRADE
  www.thefurtrapper.com.
  This Web site includes information on the Rocky Mountain fur trade that was conducted between mountain men, the Plains Indians (including Indians of the Rocky Mountains), and the fur traders of the United States and Canada.

NORTHWEST JOURNAL
  www.northwestjournal.ca.
  Articles and details on every aspect of the fur trade.

WHITE OAK SOCIETY
  www.whiteoak.org.
  Living history interpretations of the fur-trade era.

WISCONSIN HISTORICAL SOCIETY
  www.wisconsinhistory.org/topics/shorthistory/furtrade.asp.
  Short history of the fur trade as it relates to the upper Midwest.

*Active at time of publication

SUGGESTED READING

Campbell, Marjorie Wilkins. *The Nor'westers: The Fight for the Fur Trade*. Calgary, AB: Fifth House, 2002.

Durbin, William. *The Broken Blade*. New York: Delacorte Press, 1997.

Durbin, William. *Wintering*. New York: Delacorte Press, 1999.

Erdrich, Louise. *The Birchbark House*. New York: Hyperion, 1999.

Ernst, Kathleen. *Trouble at Fort La Pointe*. Middleton, WI: Pleasant Company, 2000.

Major, John S. *The Silk Route: 7,000 Miles of History*. New York: HarperCollins, 1995.

Sivertson, Howard. *The Illustrated Voyageur: Paintings and Companion Stories*. Mount Horeb, WI: Midwest Traditions, 1996.

Tanner, John. *The Falcon: A Narrative of the Captivity and Adventures of John Tanner*. New York: Penguin Books, 1994.

PLACES TO VISIT

NORTH WEST COMPANY FUR POST
A restored fur-trading post located on the Snake River in east-central Minnesota, this historic site is operated by the Minnesota Historical Society. The living-history site includes an exact reconstruction of the fur post discovered in 1932 by young Joe Neubauer, an Ojibwa camp, hiking trails, and a new visitor center and interpretive exhibit depicting the fur trade in its heyday. Call 320-629-6356 or visit *www.mnhs.org* for museum hours and more information.

GRAND PORTAGE NATIONAL MONUMENT
Part of the National Park Service, the North West Company's Grand Portage fort is on its original site at Grand Portage Bay. The fort was the largest British fur-trade outpost and depot. Located on the north shore of Lake Superior in the very northeast tip of Minnesota, the fort includes the great hall, kitchen, canoe warehouse, an Ojibwa/voyageur camp, and park service personnel dressed in period costumes. The park's trails, including the famed eight-and-one-half-mile Grand Portage, are open year-round. Call 218-387-2788 or visit *www.nps.gov/grpo/home1.htm* for more information and dates for special events.

FORTS FOLLE AVOINE HISTORICAL PARK
A project of the Burnett County Historical Society in Webster, Wisconsin, this living history site includes the reconstructed post of the North West Company as well as the nearby house of the rival XY Company. The park features an Indian village, hiking trails, and a visitor center with exhibits, library, and gift shop. Call 715-866-8890 or visit *www.theforts.org* for more information.

FORT WILLIAM HISTORICAL PARK
Old Fort William is a historic site operated by the Ontario Ministry of Tourism and Recreation. Through its living-history program, this large and historically detailed fort depicts the fur trade activities of the North West Company at the site of its inland headquarters and annual rendezvous from 1803 to 1821. This is North America's largest fur trade reconstruction, located an hour north of Grand Portage, Minnesota, in Thunder Bay, Ontario. For more information, call 807-577-8461 or visit *www.fwhp.ca/*.

COLONIAL MICHILIMACKINAC
Taken from the French by the British after the fall of New France in 1763, Fort Michilimackinac was a main center of the fur trade for over a half century. As with all the restorations listed here, each building in the reconstructed post has been painstakingly excavated, researched, and rebuilt in its original location and manner. The fort is located on the south shore of the Straits of Mackinac in Michigan. Call 231-436-4100 or visit *www.mackinacparks.com/colonial-michilimackinac* for more information.

CHAMPLAIN'S HABITATION
In 1604, Samuel de Champlain, with his colleague Pierre Du Gua de Monts and a small group of fellow adventurers, established a fur-trading colony in the New World, choosing as their base tiny Île Ste-Croix in the southwestern corner of modern-day New Brunswick, Canada. Reconstructed and furnished according to the standards and best practices then known to archaeologists, restoration architects, and material-culture specialists, the habitation was the centerpiece of Canada's new Port-Royal National Historic Site. This is one of the earliest-built heritage projects undertaken in Canada, and the community support that nurtured it showed a vibrant and growing interest in public history. Check *www.gov.ns.ca/nsarm/virtual/habitation* for information.

PLACES TO VISIT

VILLA LOUIS
Located in the Mississippi River town of Prairie du Chien, Villa Louis is the restored home
of Wisconsin fur trader Hercules Dousman. For hours and visitor information, see
www.wisconsinhistory.org/villalouis/details.asp.

FORT LARAMIE NATIONAL HISTORIC SITE
Established as a private fur-trading post in 1834, Fort Laramie, Wyoming, witnessed the westward
expansion that dominated the nineteenth century. Operated by the National Park Service, Fort
Laramie is open for visitors year-round. For further information, see *www.nps.gov/fola/planyourvisit/
hours.htm.*

FORT VANCOUVER NATIONAL HISTORIC SITE
Located in the Vancouver/Portland/Washington metropolitan area, Fort Vancouver is operated by the
National Park Service. As the administrative center and principal supply depot of the British Hudson's
Bay Company's vast Columbia Department, Fort Vancouver served as the hub of an extensive fur-
trading network utilizing two dozen posts, six ships, and about six hundred employees during peak
seasons. For operating hours and other information, check out *www.nps.gov/fova/planyourvisit/
hours.htm.*

BENT'S OLD FORT NATIONAL HISTORIC SITE
Another fur-trading post operated by the National Park Service, Bent's Old Fort National Historic
Site is a reconstructed 1840s adobe fur-trading post on the mountain branch of the Santa Fe Trail.
Traders, trappers, travelers, and Plains Indian tribes came together here to trade. Today, living
historians re-create the sights, sounds, and smells of the past with guided tours, demonstrations, and
special events. Go to *www.nps.gov/beol/planyourvisit/hours.htm* for more information.

MUSEUM OF THE FUR TRADE
The Museum of the Fur Trade is located near Chadron, Nebraska, and is "dedicated to the memory
of the traders and trappers who explored a continent, and to the Indians with whom they traded,
played, and fought." The museum is open in the summer. Hours and admission fees are listed at
www.furtrade.org/9visit.html.

FORT SNELLING
Located at the confluence of the Mississippi and Minnesota rivers, Fort Snelling is a reconstructed,
living-history museum in the heart of Minnesota's Twin Cities. The fort was completed in 1825
and became an important outpost for the U.S. Army. Today the fort is operated by the Minnesota
Historical Society. Costumed guides present a vivid picture of early military, civilian, and American
Indian life in the region. For hours and museum location, visit
events.mnhs.org/calendar/hours.cfm?VenueID=12&bhcp=1.

INDEX

Page numbers in **boldface** refer to illustrations and captions.

PICTURE CREDITS